I WAS A DRUMMER

SHE WAS A DANCER

STEVEN M THOMAS

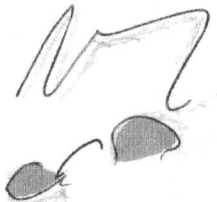

Drummer Dancer Publications

Copyright © 2016 by Steven M. Thomas.

Published by Drummer Dancer Publications

Book and photographs: Steven M. Thomas

Cover and direction: Haans Peterson

Introduction: Eric Svoboda

Other books by this author:

Chase The Rabbit

Rabbits Never Die

The Hollywood Murders

Aloha, Logosi!

Goodbye Harlow Nights

No part of this book may be reproduced or transmitted in any form or by any means, electronic or mechanical, including photocopying, recording, or by any information storage and retrieval systems, without the written permission of the publisher, expect where permitted by law.

Introduction by Eric Svoboda

I first met Steve at a party at Roger Mayden's apartment in 1985. Roger and I were in a band, **The Eighth Day**, with my childhood friend, Brian. We were destined for greatness- just a matter of all the pieces falling into place, right? So, Steve volunteered to be our manager- a piece we were missing. Great, you're in Steve, welcome to the band. It was that simple, really. I didn't really know anything about him.

After we all moved to Martha's Vineyard, we lived together for about eight months. We were, essentially, together every day for nearly two years, I think. He knew almost everything there was to know about me- I made sure he did so he could handle all of those press inquiries that would be coming his way. I mean, he'd need to know all about my childhood, my girlfriends, my favorite food, movies-all that-to be able to properly present me to the music press. And he wanted to know all that stuff-I think he really was interested. And why shouldn't he be, the world revolved around me. I was 19.

I never asked Steve about his history and, I don't think he ever volunteered much aside from trying to turn me onto **The Beatles** (so what) and **Elvis Costello** (so what) and **Jonathan Richman** (so what). So what- they didn't play synthesizers so they were boring. A bunch of old men. And Steve was older too so he had "it" all figured out for himself and for us, so that was good-I could write songs and he would do the rest. Did I mention the world revolved around me? I was 19.

Steve has talked about writing a book for as long as I've known him. It was going to be a book about the band-so, it was going to be a book about me. That was exciting. I was 21, 25, 30, 35, 40 and the world had slowly slid it's center of revolution off me during that time. But there was always the book coming that would sort of nudge it back to me someday. I looked forward to reading it.

I'm 45. Steve texted me a few months ago and said he was writing a book and that one chapter would be on **The Eighth Day**. Hmmm. That's not "the book" he'd been promising. What's this going to be about?

He emailed me an early draft right before Christmas. I was genuinely excited to finally have this. Honestly, I suppose what I intended to do (if

I'm being honest) is to read it fairly quickly, focus on all the stuff with my name on it, squeeze as much egotistical pleasure as I could from those sentences, and then tell Steve that it was really good, that I enjoyed it, loved that one part, this was funny, this was thoughtful, glad you finally did this, etc. etc. etc. That's my plan.

So, I'm off work for the holidays, make myself a drink, sit down by the fire and start reading the book from my phone…little tiny words. And as I read…shit…this is really good. Maybe my first thought is relief! Steve's the drummer, I get that. Who's the dancer-the girlfriend? Never heard of her. He was in love? (Really, more than that.) And he never mentioned her? Why not? Oh-I never asked. The world revolving and all that.

Back in the late 80's or early 90's, Steve gave me a stapled together book of computer paper (nicely assembled). Don't recall the title, but it was a bunch of his poems. One of them was called **Cardboard Box Tomb**. It was about a bad breakup after which the author couldn't bear being in certain places he's shared with his ex-lover. And he couldn't understand why they broke up, and he kept their old love letters and whatnot in a cardboard box. I liked the meter and content and used his words in a sort of rap song that I recorded at the time. Truly horrible musically, but I still know the words by heart till this day.

I made the connection quickly-this book explained that poem and much, much more. It is, certainly, a romantic declaration shouted from the proverbial mountaintop! For Steve, I imagine that writing this book has been a way for him to ask and answer questions about the moments and people that his world had revolved around. Entertaining, yes. But also, I think he's found some answers here that apply beyond his revolving world. Seems like he has some of "it" figured out, after all. Thanks, Steve, for sharing.

Eric Svoboda

Foreword

Saturday, September 8

I took my ten year old son, Justin, to the Cahokia Mounds today, located in Cahokia, Illinois, about 30 miles from where we live. It is the site of the oldest known civilization in America. The Mississippian Indians had a vast city there from 400 AD to 1400 AD. It was the size of London and was the most powerful place on the Continent. They built many great mounds, some of which are still there to this day. They held rituals attended by thousands, played drums and danced. An amazing history. There's a great museum there with many exhibits and artifacts. But while looking at an exhibit of one of the kinds of drums they made and played, it struck me like a bolt of lightning! Since the dawn of civilization, there have been drummers and dancers. There has been love and magic. Victory and joy. Loss and sorrow. That has not changed in thousands of years and likely never will. As I stood there looking at this drum with my son, it dawned on me that perhaps someday he too would plays drums, but of a different kind. He may meet a dancer, but of a different style. This story is as old as humankind. This story is mine. I was a drummer and she was a dancer.

STEVEN M THOMAS

Chapter One

Down in the basement and into the sky...

...St. Charles, Missouri 1978.

I was late getting to the party because I worked the 3:30 PM to Midnight shift at Hussmann Refrigeration Company. Not a bad gig for a 19-year-old kid. I was taking home about $250. a week, so I didn't mind the hours. Most of the college kids were gone by the time I got there, which was fine by me. I was going to see Kim Jordan, a girl I'd met not long before. Nothing else much mattered. Pat's parents were out of town, so she was hosting a little get together. Kim was making New England clam chowder from scratch, but I think it was pretty much gone by the time I got there. The college girls devoured it and went back to their dorms I guess. So it was just me and Kim, Pat and another Lindenwood College friend of ours, Roger Mayden. I don't remember how many times I'd seen Kim before that. But enough to know I was quickly falling for her. And she was crazy about me. She seemed to be on mission to win my heart, and was winning the war. I didn't even go to Lindenwood College, but hung out there from time to time over the years. But this particular night, the underlying purpose of the party was actually for me. At least as far as Kim was concerned. So I arrived late and was greeted by Kim most endearingly. She hugged me tight and whispered "I have some beer for you in the downstairs fridge!" So down we went. She had gotten me my brand! Pabst Blue-ribbon! Wow! She remembered. "I didn't want anyone to drink it," she explained. And with that, I hugged and kissed her. And in that instant, the most amazing thing happened to me. I fell madly in love with Kimberli J. Jordan of Rhode Island. It was the most profound moment of my life. And out of nowhere, these words came out of my mouth: *"I will always love you. I will never leave you."* And she wept. It was a great release for her I believe, because she had been acting very anxious and nervous. I think she was afraid I wouldn't accept her, would reject her. Instead, she got those words. And I meant them to the core of my being. It was as serious a commitment as marriage in mind. And I am proud of having said those words to this very day. We went back upstairs to join our friends and danced to an Elvis Costello album.

The story begins at the entrance to Lindenwood College, St. Charles, MO. Notice the perfectly straight line of linden trees going up the street to Sibley Hall. The building to the left is McClure Hall where Kim lived.

Four years earlier...

Right after junior high school, my parents moved me from St. Charles, Missouri to Bethalto, Illinois, of all places. My stepfather wanted to be closer to his blue-collar job at the oil refinery. Don Link was an asshole, to put it mildly. And he was from the Frank Sinatra/Dean Martin school of music. He hated rock and roll. I had to have my hair cut short all the time, which made me stick out like a sore thumb amongst my peers at the time. This was 1974. He actually told me one time that guys having long hair was "inhuman." So that was the kind of mentality from an authority figure I was having to deal with as a child. I was not at all happy about being uprooted, but such was my childhood. Every year or two, we would move it seemed. And at age 15, your friends are the most important things in your life. So it was a new school, a new neighborhood, and hopefully new friends. The summer passed and I started my sophomore year at Civic Memorial High School. We had to get to school an hour early for band, which meant I had to walk instead of taking the bus. And it was probably a mile or two. But I didn't care. I wanted to be a drummer in band! Marching band practice was first on the agenda, and I happened to be standing in formation on the football field with a very tall, kind of odd-looking clarinet player. I was very short for my age, probably 4 foot ten or something, and this kid had to be six feet! And he was a senior. I was a sophomore. But this guy was cool as hell. His name was Steve Lawton, but all the kids called him Stub. And he played bass guitar! I started going over to his house after I was finished with dinner and washing the dishes. He introduced me to his guitarist friend, Randy Wells, also a senior at the high school. They happened to have an old set of mismatched drums, and just like that, I was in a rock and roll garage band. Literally. We rehearsed in Steve's parent's detached garage! Looking back on it, we weren't that good. But we were loud and fast and played mostly original songs. And it was fun! One of Randy's older brothers set up colored floodlights in the garage, and we would play "live concerts" almost every night. Neighbors and friends would come by to cheer us on. And there were even a few girls. The second best reason to be in a band. I was fifteen and couldn't even drive yet, had short hair, and these girls were actually paying attention to me. Because I was a drummer in a rock and roll band. We were called **"The Wild Wings."** I don't think they realized the significance of the name because I think Randy came up with it. But I was very much aware that it was a spinoff of Paul McCartney's new band **Wings.** Just a coincidence I guess. **The Beatles** had been everything to me since I saw them on Ed Sullivan. But the comparisons stop there. We weren't that good, but there weren't many rock bands in Bethalto, Illinois in 1974. I only remember a few songs, probably because that's all we did. Over and over. Guitarist Randy Wells wrote most of them, but my personal favorite was by Steve Lawton. It was called **"Yesterday's Sleeper."** I still remember all the words. And Steve not only got to school an hour early for band, he got there even earlier for his part-time job gassing up the busses! It was a whirlwind year! I was in high school band, wrote for the school newspaper, took an electronics class and built a radio, ran for student council, was in the Junior Achievement program and took driver's ed and learned how to drive. And still found time for **The Wild Wings**! But as things wound down that year, and Steve and Randy were about to graduate, things got worse for me on the home front. I quietly made plans to get the hell out. So on the last day of school, I went to live with my 21-year-old sister back in St. Charles. The ploy was I would just be staying with her for the Summer. But the idea was I would not be going back to Bethalto. I enrolled in St. Charles High School and my Mother followed me soon thereafter, leaving Don Link and a relationship that spanned some six years. Our new home, as it turned out, was right next door to Lindenwood College. Sometimes I took the bus to school, but more often than not, I would walk the mile or so. And I would cut through Lindenwood campus. There was this one spot where I could slide on my back under the great, black wrought iron fence that surrounded the 150-plus year old school. It wasn't just a short cut, it was a beautiful campus, with it's grand linden trees and well manicured grass and amazing old buildings. It was the first college West of the Mississippi. I loved that place. So off I would go, sliding under the fence and make my way across campus, down to North Kingshighway to St. Charles High School. Every morning. But this time, I didn't join the school band. Instead I concentrated on the school newspaper. Those two years of high school seemed like a damned eternity in a way. But I wrote a lot. We had a mimeographed daily "paper" called **"The Daily Thing"** and I wrote quite a bit for that, plus the regular student newspaper. And did a bit of work on the yearbook.

Working in the high school journalism office my junior year, 1976. I look like a blonde Ramone. They put this photo in the yearbook. Someone turned on a tape recorder and asked "Is there anything else you would like to add Mr. Thomas?"

Veita Jo Hampton was my journalism teacher, and she was a big influence on me at the time. She knew everything about journalism and photography and pushed me to be a better writer. It was the only class I took seriously. And I excelled at it. But I was a bit more of a rebel, I guess, than the other students. My Senior year especially. I had always been kind of cocky because I knew I was good at writing and thought I was more creative than the rest of the kids. And I was. I could write straight news stories and poetry with both hands at the same damn time. I knew about music other than what was being played on the local pop radio stations. I didn't give a rat's ass about sports or academics. I found the whole high school experience to be insulating and stifling, and despite all that, or perhaps because of that, I was well liked and respected by teacher Miss Hampton and the other journalism students. There was Barb Ulsamer, Deana Tucker, Mike Snelling, and a handful of others. They made me "Original Composition Editor" for the school paper. I didn't even ask for that. And it sucked because that meant I had to decide whose poetry would go into the little poetry section of the newspaper each month. So everyone had to submit their poems to me. And I had to read them. I was so self absorbed into my own poetry that it was hard to be objective, so I just printed almost everything that was given to me, whether I liked it or not. How are you going to judge poetry anyway, I thought? There are no rules with poetry. I thought most of it was really bad, and it probably was, but then again, mine probably was too. Besides English class, journalism was the only class that mattered to me, the only one where I felt like I was doing something. I loved writing for **The Daily Thing** because I could go to school one day, write something that same day, and see it in print the following day. Immediate gratification. It went beyond the typical high school bullshit. I felt like I was doing something other than making B's in all the classes I didn't care about. I did a story on a teacher's strike that no one else would have thought about covering, even though it directly affected all of us.

The biggest story I wrote never got published. It was about two friends of mine who were selling pot part-time. This was 1977. I did not reveal their names, of course, but did an interview with them and a subsequent feature piece where they revealed that they sold pot and made a little money, "enough to pay my car insurance" one of them was quoted as saying. When I turned the story in for publication in the school paper, Miss Hampton called me down to talk to the school vice-principal, Mr. John Maxwell to have a little talk with me. And as you can imagine, they wanted me to tell them the names of the two students. "As a journalist," I told them, "I can not reveal my sources." I was serious about it. The story never got printed. It was one of the best exposes of a high school paper and they sat on it for obvious political purposes. It was suppression of the press. They didn't pressure me to reveal my sources. They respected that but did not allow the story to go out. I felt it was hypocritical. But I understand it now. High school is not the real world. That's partly why I was anxious for it to be over. They were teaching me about journalism, but when I practiced it, and actually produced a story that had some substance, they sat on it because I would not reveal my sources. The two guys that I wrote the story about weren't big drug dealers, but they sold a bit of pot. I bought from them for Christ's sake, that's how I knew! They were just St. Charles High School students who made good grades and so forth. And they trusted me to do a tape recorded interview.

We did it in Kevin Smith's basement and they knew it was for a story I would write. I promised not to reveal their names, and they respected me enough to go along with it. That speaks volumes.

So I had a bit of a reputation after that with everyone. Students, teachers and the administration. I wasn't writing about the latest football game. I wasn't there to help build the Homecoming float either. But when it came time to write a poem, they also thought of me. I didn't work much on the yearbook, but there was a kid who took some photos of the Missouri River, and I was asked to write a poem to go along with the pictures. It may have been Barb Ulsamer. She was the editor of the school paper and a pretty good friend. I kind of had a crush on Barb. She was a bit of a rebel like me. She had a boyfriend who went to a different High School, so we were never really boyfriend/girlfriend, but Barb was the closest person to me female-wise in high school. So I went over to Barb's house one night while they were having one of their yearbook meetings. I looked at the photographs the kid had taken and sat down, and in ten minutes wrote a poem. It was called **"God, There's Life On The River."**

I think they just wanted to have something of mine in the yearbook, I don't know.

I was honored that they asked me, but I was in and out of there in an hour or less. I never really hung out with them that much outside of school. I really liked Barb though. Even took her to our Senior Prom. But I never had a girlfriend in high school.

I bought a used set of drums in 1976. A five-piece mother of pearl set of Pearl drums for $150. I worked part-time at a music store and actually taught percussion. So although I wasn't in the high school band, I still played music. Part of me felt like I'd gone passed that high school band stuff when I'd already done the **Wild Wings** at age fifteen. And I didn't care for pop music of the time. I wasn't aware of it then, but I was very much at the crust of what would soon become "punk rock" or "new wave." No one had really made much of an influence on me since **The Beatles**. I wasn't interested otherwise. I played music in the basement with my old friend Kevin Smith, and also my best friend Mark Snow. Man, Mark remained a great friend of mine. He stuck with me through thick and thin and remains a great friend to this very day.

We played **Alice Cooper**'s **"I'm Eighteen," Chuck Berry**'s **"Johnny B. Goode,"** and **The Beatles "And I Love Her."** We probably did a few others, but those we did over and over.

Later, after Mark sort of dropped out, Kevin and I did **"Johnny B. Goode,"** and **Rush's "Bastille Day"** and a few songs I'd written. But we were a two-piece and not really a band. I literally didn't know anyone else at the time who would have been interested in playing anything other than what I considered to be pure drivel. Then one day I picked up a copy of **Rolling Stone** magazine and it had **The Sex Pistols** on the cover. And Holy Shit! What was this? They were doing something that seemed like true rebellion. Rock and roll. Their album wasn't yet available, but I quickly went out and pre-ordered it. Just based on the story, it sounded like it would be great. And as it turns out, it was. Elvis Costello quickly followed, and I thought "Oh my God! This is great! Something is actually happening that I like!"

The album came into the store that I had preordered it from, and me and a few friends, including Haans Peterson, immediately loved it. Kevin followed suit and we started learning the songs. This seemed important to us. The rest of the world caught up many years later, but by then it was too late. Our senior year ended, and it was time to go off to college somewhere. I'd earned a last minute small scholarship for coming in second place in State for a feature story I had written about a kid who got expelled from St. Charles High School in 1971 for having his hair too long. So off I went to The University of Missouri-Columbia, one of the top journalism schools in the Nation. But not long after moving into the dorms, I couldn't stand the place. It was a huge campus and all I had was a ten-speed bicycle. And I had to take freshman level classes that really seemed like a step backwards to me. And forget about writing for the school paper. You couldn't even walk into the office when you were a freshman. I hated it and dropped out before the first semester ended. I went back home and got a job at Hussmann, where my new stepfather Bob worked. And that's when I started hanging around Lindenwood College a bit more.

I played music with my old high school friend, Kevin Smith and continued to write. On weekends, I started going to **"The Rocky Horror Picture Show"** where I met some pretty interesting people, including a kid who went by the name Michael Foxx. We would hang out before and after the show, which didn't start until midnight, so most of the time I didn't get home until the sun was coming up. We dreamed of starting a band and played music in his cassette stereo car player. But like a lot of young men, we didn't really have a plan. I was shooting from the hip in the dark. We never actually got around to playing music together. But we talked about it at length. One night Michael brought his sister to the show, and he was very protective of her. Eventually, I stopped going. It had kind of ran its course with me. I ran into a mutual friend a few months later named Joe, and he told me Michael had moved to New York and was playing in a band called **"Bad Habits."** I had lost touch with him, but we had been friends who shared a common interest in new music and I knew he was quite compassionate about it. We never did play music together though. Michael Foxx, as it turns out, moved with his family back to Georgia, where he finally started a group called **R.E.M.** Turns out his real name was Michael Stipe. I didn't put it together that this was the same guy for almost twenty years.

One day my oldest and best friend, Haans Peterson, and I were hanging out at Lindenwood and we met a girl named Pat Pfaff and her friend Cathy. Haans and Pat hit it off right away. She liked him because was an artist. Cathy was a very cute girl and a gifted musician. But I wasn't so lucky. Cathy had other guys interested in her, and didn't quite understand me. And musically, we were miles apart. I brought **The Runaways** live album over to the house that Cathy was staying at, where about 3 or 4 other college girls were living off campus. I had just discovered **The Runaways** myself. Their story is well documented, but at the time, in the Midwest at least, they weren't that well known. They were the first all-girl rock and roll group, of course, and I played the album and Cathy loved the song **Cherry Bomb!** Maybe I had taught her something after all.

Soon after, I met another Lindenwood College girl. Pat set me up with her.

"Hi, I'm Kim," she said rather shyly.

"Nice to meet you, I am Steve," I replied. How do you go from that to "I will always love you, I will never leave you?" And mean it.

Chapter Two

The only thing I was sure about was that I loved Kim Jordan. That was all that mattered. The rest of the story is just details.

Sibley Hall, Lindenwood College. This was the first building at Lindenwood and is still a girl's dorm, just as it was when I met Kim in 1978. Pat Paff lived there at the time, and Haan's did a giant painting on her dorm room wall. The school painted over it the following year.

I wish I could tell you exactly when and where I first met Kim. It was probably at a small party I went to one night held at the home of a lady professor from Lindenwood. We sat on the floor in this old house that had a historic marker on the front of it. The lady professor was an older woman and very cool. I looked through her record collection and found The Beatle's <u>White Album</u> and quickly put it on the turntable. Kim was immediately taken to me. I could see it in her eyes. I wasn't sure why, of course, but I wasn't about to question it. We talked about music, and she told me that she was from a small village called Wickford in Rhode Island, where she grew up. She said she chose Lindenwood because she loved the way the campus looked. I could totally relate to that. After all, I'd been going there for years. I just never bothered taking classes.

Later that night I walked her home to her dorm, McClure Hall, and as we were approaching the building, a male voice yelled out "Kim! Get in here!" As I recall, he hollered that out through a window of the building. He may have been in her room, I didn't know. I thought, "holy shit, she has a boyfriend and he is pissed off!" I let her walk the rest of the way by herself, and I could hear him reading her the riot act. I thought "Well, that's too bad. I really, really liked that girl." But later in the week, I saw her again, and never heard anything else about the other guy. So I am not sure what happened and quite frankly, I didn't really care. Somehow, he was out of the picture. I'm guessing he broke up with her. Maybe that night.

This is the sidewalk next to McClure Hall where Kim and I walked down one night shortly after meeting. Some guy from inside the building yelled "Kim! Get in here!"

I might have met her for the second time at dancer concert. Her and a few other dancer students had to choreograph and perform a dance piece for their final grade, and one of the other girls was my friend Pat Pfaff. Pat invited Haans and I to come watch. So we went. And it was absolutely awful! It appeared as though all of the dancers, and I think there were four, were just doing their own thing. It was obvious that very little thought went into it. But Kim was doing ballet, and it was great! I don't know what the hell the others were doing, but Kim was doing ballet stuff! Then the dance teacher started giving her critique, and all I remember of that is her saying "Kim, we don't teach ballet here." What the hell? I understood the riff between modern and classical dance, but I had never seen this kind of prejudice first hand. That's all I remember about that meeting. The first time I walked into Kim's dorm was to see her clothes. She had these great skirts. They were dance skirts that were literally split down one side and tied around the waist. I didn't realize they were dance skirts. She probably told me, but I had never seen anything like them before. It was almost her entire wardrobe. She wore dance clothes all the time. She showed me each one with pride, and I was genuinely interested and impressed. And the girl was definitely out to impress me. But the most intriguing thing in her room was taped to her wall above her bed.

She had handwritten the lyrics to the song

"Sunshine." I was blown away. ***"If he can't even run his own life, I'll be damned if he'll run mine. Sunshine!"*** She was no doubt referring to the old boyfriend, and I think she even told me so. It was very powerful and also very ironic. Seven years previously, I had gone to my first school dance. I was in the 7th grade and there was a live band. I had never seen a live rock band like that before. And that was the same year I'd taught myself how to play a full set of drums. Our school had one. And the drummer in this band also sang while he played drums. That was very rare to see anywhere. And this guy sang **"Sunshine."** I never told her that story. It was almost like a sign. Out of all of the song lyrics in history, there it was on her wall. **"Sunshine."** It was an incredible coincidence. And it wouldn't be the last.

McClure Hall Lindenwood College, where Kim lived when I first met her. The first time I walked into her dorm was to see her clothes. And I noticed a song lyric she had copied down and had taped to her wall. It was called "Sunshine" and it blew me away.

Kim was a beautiful blonde haired girl, and very young, my age, 19 or 20 at the time we met. She had amazing features. A face like an angel, fragile yet strong. There was something about her eyes. Sometimes there was a glimmer of tragedy in her eyes, and at times when the light was just right, I could see into her soul. I really believed that. And I could tell in an instant if she was happy or sad. Almost from the start, I could tell how she was feeling by looking into her eyes, even when she was trying to hide it. It is an instinctive phenomena that only happens between people who love each other. I don't know the science behind it, but I know it exists. She would try to mask her feelings sometimes. She was a dancer. That is how she expressed herself. And she lived liked one. I was falling for her. But I was a bit concerned about that. After all, she lived in Rhode Island. A thousand miles away! I didn't want to say goodbye, but I knew that day was coming at the end of the semester. But she would be back, I thought. It hurt to think she would be leaving. A Summer was forever. I wanted to go with her. I even thought about asking her if I could do that. But her parents would never go for that. It was a crazy thought. But when you are 20 and in love, crazy thoughts like that enter your mind. You just don't share them with anyone other than the person you are in love with. It just wouldn't make sense to anyone else.

We were driving somewhere one time and Kim said "I love the way you talk!" I was commenting about something and used the term "to the max!" She loved that. She loved those little things about me. She loved the way I talked.

My good friend from high school, Jim Koksal and I aquired a two-bedroom apartment in a new well to do community about 15 miles west of St. Charles called Lake St. Louis. They had a huge lake; it might as well have been the damn ocean to us, and a 9-hole golf course. We had to lie about our age on the leasing form. We had my old upright piano in the living room and my friend Haan's had loaned us some of his paintings. I bought an antique bedroom set. It was quite an impressive layout for two young men like us. Sometimes we would stay up partying all night and then go play golf as the sun came up. We smoked pot, but not all the time.

We both worked, and had about ten irons in various fires at the same time. Haans had broken up with Pat, and Jim was there to scoop her up. So one night Pat brought Kim to our bachelor pad. They ended up spending the night. And that was the night I lost my virginity to Kim. I never told her that either.

The first time I brought Kim to Lake St. Louis, she took one look at the water that went on forever and said "Oh look! Sailboats!" It reminded her of home back in Wickford.

Kim showed up at our apartment one night for some reason, and I don't recall the circumstances surrounding that. She was worried about me for some reason, and since she didn't have a car, she begged and finally wore down a fellow girl student to let her use her car to come see me. She just wanted to see me. Our friend Pat later told me that Kim was desperate to see me and went on and on about it so much that her friend finally relented and let her borrow her car. Kim wanted me, period. I thought that was the greatest thing that I'd ever heard. And it was.

I had just bought a mono copy of **"Meet The Beatles"**, and was playing the hell out of it in the apartment. Kim told me that she didn't like the song **"You Can't Do That."** "Why not?" I asked. "It's one of the best Lennon vocals of all time." "The lyrics," she replied. I hadn't even thought of that!

"Well it's the second time I caught you talking to him, if I have to tell you one more time I think it's a sin, I'm gonna let you down and leave you flat! Because I told you before, oh! You can't do that!" It was blatantly chauvinistic. All I heard was the incredible vocal. I didn't really think about it. Kim was listening to the words.

Late one Friday night, there was a knock at the door, I looked through the peephole and saw some guy in jeans and a white t-shirt standing there that I didn't know. So I opened the door and all hell broke loose. Six uniformed cops with their guns drawn rushed into the apartment! "Get down on the floor" they yelled! It was crazy! My friend Kevin Smith was there with me and Jim, having arrived only minutes before. We were being busted for drugs! Oddly enough, we didn't have any drugs! They had us sit on the couch, handcuffed while they turned our apartment upside down. All they found were a couple of egg cartons of two-inch pot plants Jim had in the windowsill of his bedroom. They were pissed. For some reason, they thought we were big drug dealers and had woken a judge to get a warrant to search our apartment. So they arrested us on "cultivation" charges. A felony. Off to jail we went, and since it was a Friday night, we couldn't post bail until Monday morning.

The **Lake St. Louis Times** ran a story on it, complete with a photo of the Chief of Police sitting next to the tiny pot plants they had confinscated from our apartment. And a scale that belonged to Jim, who was a big science buff. He had an old scale that used weights on one side to measure ounces, grams, etc. The headline was **"Biggest Drug Bust in Lake St. Louis History!"** The story went on to explain that when these tiny two inch pot plants were fully grown, they would have yielded such and such amount of sellable pot, and I believe they even put a resale street value on it! It was a witch hunt. We found out later that the guy who lived upstairs from us was a retired reported. Apparently he had been walking his dog and saw the little pot plants in Jim's window sill. He subsequently tipped off the police and made us out to be major drug dealers. Apparently they believed him. He wrote the story for the **Lake St. Louis Times**. That's how it came down. The police should have busted him for lying. It was a giant shit sandwich for everyone, but Jim and I were about to take the biggest bite.

I am holding up the first check I ever got for writing. $135. for writing articles and news stories for The Lake St. Louis Times. Ironically, the same newspaper that ran the blown-out-ofproportion story on my Lake St. Louis drug bust a few years earlier. Justice is sweet.

That night, and it was really late by then, they let me make a phone call, so I called my sister Tina. She said she would put her house up for bail. I was afraid to call my parents. Since this happened on a Friday night, I couldn't get out until the following Monday. So I spent the entire weekend in a jail cell. When we were finally brought to court, we were in handcuffs and had to sit in the section reserved for criminals. It was incredibly demeaning. My Mother and sister picked Kim up at Lindenwood because she absolutely insisted on going to the arraignment. Somehow Kim had found out what had happened, probably from Pat, and called my sister Tina in a panic. She called her several times trying to figure out how I would be bailed out of jail. Kim was frantic, my sister said. And my sister had to go back home and wake up her husband Earl and drag him down to court because he also had to sign the papers to get me out because his name was on the mortgage of their house. I had to go back to jail and wait some more, and my Mother and Kim waited together. Then, finally, **All Rise!**

Apparently my baby niece, Mary Elizabeth, found the string on Kim's cool wrap around dress and Kim nearly lost her skirt in the courtroom as she stood up! Baby Mary started getting fussy, and it was Kim who picked her up and took her outside of the courtroom. My Mother and sister were too numb to leave the courtroom. My Mother later recounted how she saw Kim through the courtroom windows, carrying Mary up and down the street. It meant a great deal to my Mother to see that, she said. Kim cared. We drove home with me and Kim in the backseat, and she held me and talked about how stupid and unfair the whole thing was. I just remember thinking "I am so lucky to have this support," from my family and from Kim. She really loved me. We went to my parent's house and ate. My sister said that our Mother felt the need to feed me.

Sometimes it takes a tragedy to bring people closer together. Kim shared with me a real tragedy that had happened in her life years earlier that put my problems into perspective. She had lost her older brother. He died in an automobile accident at a very young age. She didn't tell me many details, but he was a few years older than her. I couldn't even imagine what she had gone through by losing her brother. I don't remember if she told me his name. I didn't ask any questions. I didn't know what to say. When I think really hard about it, I can still see that tragedy in her eyes as she recounted her loss. She bared her soul to me and I could see it in her eyes. Her eyes showed everything.

This girl loved me and I had to do something about it. I had already told her "I will always love you, I will never leave you," but I had to prove that. She was about to go back home for the Summer. I decided I needed to give her a ring to go back with. Not an engagement ring, but a promise ring. I felt I owed her that. A promise.

Jim and I left the apartment and moved back home. He didn't want to move, and couldn't understand why I felt it was necessary. He actually enjoyed his time in jail, he said. It inspired him somehow. It was a nightmare for me. I had to pay a lawyer $800. to get me out of hot water. His name was Rudy Beck. My sister found him for me. The charges were dropped to a mere misdemeanor possession charge. I had to serve 40 hours of community service work. And I talked to my Mother about getting Kim a ring. My Mother said, "Yes, let me see what we have here," and opened her jewelry box that she'd had ever since I could remember. She pulled out a very beautiful ring that looked like a little engagement ring. "This belonged to your grandmother," she said. "You should give this to Kim." Amazing! It was perfect. Not only a very pretty, classic ring, but a family heirloom! I carefully put it in a ring box and made arrangements to see Kim at her dorm one night after work. I was nervous as hell.

Mclure Hall where Kim lived was always locked and there was a desk in the lobby where a student would sit at to buzz guests in. You had to tell them who you were there to see and they would call the room. When I arrived that night, Kim came out into the hallway to greet me. We actually sat in the wide hallway near her room and talked for a few minutes, and then I kissed her. And as I did, I slipped the box with the ring in it into her hand. "What is this?" she asked. She opened the box and immediately started crying. "It's a promise ring," I said. We were in love, she was overjoyed, and on that night, we were officially. . . a couple.

I had never been to a family planning office before, but I went one day with Kim, and it was strange. I was probably 20, but I didn't feel like a grown up, and here we were meeting with a counselor about having safe sex. Kim had given me the heads up, so I think she had done it before. Part of the deal was she had to have a pelvic exam, which she hated. And they gave us condoms. "Just take them," she whispered to me, "we don't have to use them, but just take them anyway." She got free birth control pills that way.

I took Kim to The Plantation Dinner Theater on one of our earliest dates. The play was Neil Simon's **"Same Time Next Year."** It was a big deal for us. I don't think I had ever been to a dinner theater before. And I want to say my Mother suggested it, but I can' be sure. It was a magical night. We got a carafe of wine, with the name of the dinner theater embossed on the glass. She kept it as a souvenir. It was a special night for us. By then, we could have powered a city with love.

We were invited by one of Kim's college friends to her house for dinner one night. I don't remember the girl's name, but she was really nice, but seriously overweight. She had her own apartment just down the street from Lindenwood, and I think her "boyfriend" lived with her. Kim explained that she really felt sorry for this girl because she was pretty sure the guy was cheating on her. He was just using her for her apartment. He made an incredible dinner of stuffed chicken breast though. I was impressed by that. Then we up the street to a bar to hear Cathy's band play music. We danced and had a great time.

Kim pulled me aside and asked me to ask the friend to dance. She hadn't danced all night. So of course, I did, but the girl said no thank you. Kim had a heart like that.

She had a part-time job in the first ever distribution office in St. Charles for the **St. Louis Post-Dispatch**. She even got my Mother a job there. The lady that ran the office was also a blonde, and probably in her thirties. Kim idolized her. She was very much in charge, and I think Kim wanted to be like that someday. We went to her house one night for some sort of a staff party. There was a young man there that worked for her as well, and he kissed her ass unashamedly. She was a very attractive woman, but she also had power. I thought she sometimes played on that a little too much. Soon after, they closed the office. Maybe she wasn't as in charge as everyone thought after all.

Kim told me she was going to transfer from

Lindenwood College to a nearby school called Webster College in St. Louis. They had an amazing dance and theater department, so I guess she realized that if she was going to be serious about getting a degree in dance, she'd better go to a school that was known for that, and not just a pretty campus. She wanted me to keep my job at Hussmann, but I hated it, and told her "I want to go to Webster with you."

Truth is, I'd have gone anywhere to be with her.

The time came for her father to come pick her up and take her back home for the Summer. We so dreaded that day. I spent the night with her in McClure Hall. I don't think I had ever done that before. We made love that night knowing it would be the last time we would see each other for nearly three months. And that was a long time, especially when you're that young. Those days were like dog years in a way. You crammed seven years into one, and everything you did was a big deal.

She was very emotionally upset that morning. It was a rough departure. I met her Dad for the first time. Al Jordan was a very nice man. He didn't know me from Adam, but apparently she had talked to her parents about me. I helped them pack their car, and watched them drive off campus, make a right onto First Capitol Drive until I lost sight of her. "Well, this is it," I thought. I shed a few tears, then went home and started writing.

Chapter Three

It struck me like lightening and happened just that quickly. I couldn't think of words worthy enough of how I was feeling. In just a few minutes, my life would be changed forever. It was like The Beatles.

Summer 1979:

The first thing I did after Kim left was started writing and recording songs for what would become a demo tape called **"boyfriend."** I had an Aikai reel-to-reel recorder and a Sony stereo cassette recorder. A guitar, a set of drums, a piano, and a lot of inspiration. I used the old Buddy Holly method of two-track recording live.

That meant I would play the song on guitar and sing and record that on the reel-to-reel, then jack that track into the cassette player and record along with it. The result was called "overdubbing." I wanted to send Kim a collection of songs as soon as possible. An album of sorts. So I worked quickly. I am guessing it took me only a couple of weeks to write and record ten or so songs. Maybe less. I didn't use anyone else. It was much faster that way. I would write something and record it that same day. I continued to play music with Kevin Smith and a few other people, but this was sort of my solo project for Kim.

I'll be the first to admit that I am not a great musician. Or singer, or songwriter. But these songs were definitely from the heart. I wish I still had that tape today. Some of them, as songs, weren't bad. I had been "writing and recording songs" for a long time. They were often crude and out of tune. Yet they were passionate and from the heart, and therefore meant a great deal to me. **"boyfriend"** was one of my best efforts up to that time.

The year before, I had bought a really old upright piano for $100. from a farmhouse estate in St. Charles. It had to be from the 30's or 40's. It was sprayed with that awful speckled crap popular in that time. I stripped it down to bare wood, which was a long process. Then I sanded, stained and varnished it. The damn thing weighed a ton, but was fairly decent sounding. I had no idea how to play piano, but was inspired by John Lennon's **Plastic Ono Band** album. He didn't know how to play piano properly either, but he did it anyway. I found middle "C" and worked from there. My fingers had the rhythm of a drummer and I quickly found ways of constructing note progressions. I used three fingers of my right hand to play chords and single notes and usually only one finger of my left hand to play bass notes. About as simple as it gets. As I experimented, songs came out. I was a drummer, and approached playing the piano from that perspective.

A lot of it was instinctive and primitive. I wrote and recorded four piano songs: **"Before I Fall," "Most Of My Money," "Real Big Deal,"** and **"Mirror Of Mistakes."** This was pre-Kim. So I had done some home recordings previous to **"boyfriend"** for Kim. I used the same double-tracking method of recording with an acoustic guitar on a song I wrote called **"A Lover And A Friend"** around the same time as the piano songs. That had been inspired in part by all of the love stories that I had ever heard before. But honestly, it was also based on my experience with a girl I had met in the neighborhood named Jeannie Ickenroth. It was actually a pretty good composition, looking back on it. The obvious theme of all of these songs was lost love and rejection. Pretty sad really. But **"A Lover And A Friend"** was one I will never forget. Another guitar song was called **"Girls Go On."** My friend Haans liked that one too. It could have been a double-sided single in the life and times of Steven Thomas circa 1978.

I finished writing and recording **"boyfriend"** and was anxious to send it off to Kim.

I mailed her that cassette tape in a nice little package. I handmade a red, heart shaped box, like a valentine's candy box. Using red construction paper, I cut out strips for the sides, top and bottom and very carefully shaped it and glued it together. It was not a perfect box. But that was the idea. It took time and care. I used paper clips and tooth picks to hold it together while the Elmer's glue dried. Then I made a little booklet with the lyrics to each song out of red paper, and hand wrote each song on the pages. And I hand stitched those pages together using a needle and red thread. Everything had to be handmade. In the bottom of the box, under the cassette and lyric booklet, I placed a red-laced garter belt. On the lid of the box, I just handwrote **"boyfriend"** all in lower case. It was the most personal and romantic piece of art I have ever created before or since. And it was made for and inspired by its only recipient, my girlfriend Kim Jordan.

Out of all of those songs on that tape, there are only a few that I remember now. It was a long time ago, and the tape was lost along with so many other physical artifacts over these years. One was called **"Now"** and it stands out in my mind for a number of reasons. I was only 20 years old, but I was writing like I'd had the foresight of a 40-year-old man. I was somehow projecting way into the future, and it is a bit haunting in retrospect. It is not lost on me that the lyrics still stand up and actually make more sense ***now*** than when I'd written it. It is ironic because I still feel the same way 33 years later, and all of that time gives the words that much more meaning. I stand by those lyrics to this day. And I am quite proud of it actually.

Now

The things I've seen and done before

Don't seem to matter anymore

I'm different now and so are things

Names and dates all change

But when you see me staring off

And wonder what I'm thinking of

It's doubtful that I'm in the past

Vague memories through the broken glass

Names and dates all change, indeed. That is life, isn't it? Time goes on and people come and go. And now is more important than then. The one name, however, would stay the same. Kim Jordan. That is it. Other names and dates all change. It may be the best love song I've ever written.

Another song I remember was called **"Shades Of Blue."** Keep in mind, I am pulling these lyrics out of my memory more than 30 years after I wrote them. The idea behind the song was just that I missed Kim and didn't want to be away from her. We were a thousand miles apart, so I pictured myself going up into the sky so I could get a view of the country, and maybe see her. I was so much in love, I could hardly function day to day without her. She wrote daily letters to cope and get through it. I wrote songs.

The only song on that tape that wasn't a love song was one called **"Underground."** It was about the stupid Lake St. Louis drug bust. And it was probably the best "pop" song on the tape. I played electric guitar, double tracked vocals and drums on that. The verses were sort of rapped, before I knew what rap was.

Like Kim with dance and gymnastics, writing lyrics came to me very early in life.

I wrote my very first song at age six while on the swing set in my backyard. It was called **"Dinoland."** My Mother had taken me along with her to a shopping mall, and they had an exhibit of life sized dinosaurs on display in the parking lot. So me being six, I imagined what it would be like if they existed in our time, right now.

Right around that time, my Mother took me to the Captain Eleven and The Three Stooges Show. It was a popular local TV kids program where this old Steamship Captain had kids on board his Mississippi river paddleboat, and they played Three Stooges shorts. I loved that show, and when they told me I was actually going to be on it, I was thrilled!

So I was looking for the boat as we drove downtown. To my surprise, instead of getting on the boat, we walked into a tall building and went up an elevator! We came to a big room, and there it was. A fake set of the inside of the boat! And there was a model of the boat, about three feet long on the set that they would show during the show. "So this isn't real?" I thought. "And where are The Three Stooges?" I still had fun, but that was quite the reality check for a six-year-old boy. Grown-ups lie, I thought. Who can you trust if you can't trust grown-ups?

A couple of years later, I got my first paying gig as a drummer. I had a friend from school named Zachary and he had a box guitar. That's an acoustic guitar. And my Aunt Cona had brought me back a set of bongos from a trip she'd taken to Mexico. So we got together and played music. He didn't even know any chords, but could hold some strings down and strum and I would keep rhythm on the bongos. It sounded sort of like slide guitar. He would sing. And he came up with this little tune called **"I Got A Lot Of You."** It went something like

Aint got a lot of money

Aint got a lot of dues

Aint got a lot of nothing

But I got a lot of you

And it went on from there, several verses.

One day we were playing that song while sitting on a street corner in our neighborhood when a man walked by and stopped to listen. When we were done playing the song, the man gave us a quarter. "Wow." I thought, "you can earn money doing this?" It was a new concept for me. We were seven years old. Other kids sold lemonade. We played music.

I got my own box guitar a few years later, and started learning proper chords from a book. But my fingers were tiny and it was hard to hold the strings down to make it sound right. Acoustic guitars are much more difficult to hold down than electric guitar strings. My fingertips would swell up on the ends and bleed. It hurt. You had to be damn well committed to play a box guitar when you were eleven. But that's all I had, so that's what I did.

As childhood went on, I would write songs and the music would be in my head. Translating that music from my mind to actual audible notes was difficult. We had a cheap little organ, and I would play around with that. It was easier to play than a guitar. After being overcome by the musical **"Jesus Christ, Superstar,"** I decided I would write an opera on the life and times of John The Baptist. I had no idea what I was doing, but wrote several songs towards that end before abandoning the idea. The opera would end in the beheading of John. I thought that would be very dramatic.

I finally got an electric guitar when I was about thirteen. I bought it from the Ben Franklin Five and Dime store on West Clay. It cost around $35. and came with a little amplifier. And I played the hell out of it. I still have that guitar.

I enlisted a friend of mine from school to play

drums for me a few times. Scott Bickle had a full set of drums. It was pretty rare to have a drum kit at age thirteen in those days. And he could keep a beat, but had trouble with fills or anything other than a straight four four beat on the bass drum.

I was actually a better drummer than he was, but I had to play guitar and sing and needed a drummer, so I took what I could get and was lucky to have him. I'd written a song called **"The Individuals,"** and we played that.

Shortly after hooking up with Scott, I made my other friend, Mark Snow, aware of what we were doing. And Mark wanted in. Mark, as it turns out, was also a huge Beatles fan. And he also had an electric guitar! And a piano! And he could play! Way better than me. So I would go over to his house after school and we became fast friends. We didn't know anyone else who shared our deep fascination with **The Beatles** and rock music in general. He had an older counsel type stereo record player in his room. The kind that was almost as big as a couch in a wood cabinet. It was a piece of furniture, really. But with that, we could play our guitars, and jack in a microphone and record. I had written a song called **"My Neighbor's Son,"** so we worked on and recorded that.

I remember the days of having fun

Always fighting with my neighbors son

Playing soldier and killing everyone

I don't remember the other lyrics. But it went on to describe the harsh realities of playing soldier and actually being one. The idea of the song was that I had this (fictional) older kid who lived next door to me who would be very nice and play war games with me, then he goes off to Vietnam for real when he turns 18 and dies when I was like 10 years old, so the concept and consequences of war becomes real. And it is my neighbor's son. Because then I have to deal with, as a 10 year old child, this man, my neighbor's loss. I would feel guilty that we were "playing" war in his backyard, and he would lose his son to the real war in Vietnam. I wrote that when I was about 13, around 1972.

So Mark Snow joined me and Scott to play music in Scott's basement. We did my song **"The Individuals,"** and Mark wanted to do **"Rocky Raccoon"** from **The Beatle's White Album**. He wanted to sing it too, so I let him. He was doing my song, so I went along with it. The annual talent show was coming up at Jefferson Junior High School, and I talked Mark and Scott into trying out for it. They were reluctant. Especially Mark, but he finally agreed to go along. I had also written a new song called **"Only If You Cared"** and we were playing that.

The try-outs were a disaster because our guitars weren't in tune, and the music teacher immediately stopped us. This was in a roomful of students watching us, so it was pretty embarrassing. There's a lot of peer pressure in junior high school. Another kid who knew how to tune a guitar was dispatched by the music teacher to help me get my guitar in working order, and we went on with our audition. But I think by then, nerves had gotten the best of Mark and Scott, so it was just a bad experience for them.

I didn't particularly care. It didn't bother me that much. So I don't have perfect pitch and couldn't tune a guitar properly. So what. I wasn't about to let that stop me. I could write a damn song, *so listen to this*, I thought.

Mark and Scott bailed on me. Mark told me soon after that they would not be doing the talent show with me. It was one thing to be playing music in Mark's bedroom or in Scott's basement, but an entirely different thing to be doing it in front of the whole school. I had mixed emotions about that. I was actually very troubled by it, because I thought, "well, if you think it is that bad, why are you doing it?" And it wasn't that bad, really.

Maybe it wasn't that good, but it wasn't perhaps that bad. I didn't know. But it didn't stop me. My two friends had decided it was too embarrassing to do. I decided to go it alone. So I wrote a song I could do by myself on acoustic guitar called **"Talkin' On The Telephone."**

I went back to audition by myself, got a spot in the talent show, and did that damn song. I was the only one to perform an original composition in the show, and I did it as a solo. Mark and Scott didn't come. I didn't blame them though. And just before playing, I had some other kid tune my guitar for me. My parent's didn't come either because I didn't bother telling them about it. I walked by myself with my guitar to the school that night to do the show.

While I was writing **"boyfriend,"** Kim was writing me letters nearly everyday. That is when I became very familiar with the return address on her envelopes of 141 Main Street, Wickford, Rhode Island. It became a magical place to me. Those letters were filled with what she was doing: working as a waitress, going to the beach by herself to lay out and tan, but mostly how much she loved me and couldn't wait to get back to me. They were incredible love letters. We were lovesick. I had heard of that, but I had never experienced it. It is real.

Being lovesick is when you are so much in love that you feel physically ill when you are not with that person. That may sound crazy, and maybe it is, but that is exactly what was going on with Kim and I the Summer of 1979. That feeling can defy rational reasoning. It takes you over, and no one else but the person you are in love with can understand or relate to it. It is magic. And when both of you feel that same way at the exact same time, it is called lovesick. No one else can understand it. You don't even understand it. But you have to cope with life's everyday existence. So you go on, being misunderstood by everyone in the world, except for that one person who you love and who shares that same existence. Only you two understand. And you don't even try to explain it to the rest of the world. Only you two matter anyway. And you two would deal with the rest of the world as best you could.

Sometimes we would talk on the phone. But in those days, long distance calls were pretty expensive. So there weren't that many. She wrote so many letters, I had to go out and buy one of those large cardboard boxes that fit under a bed just to keep them all together.

I wrote her too, but couldn't keep up with her. It was like she was writing a daily diary in the form of a letter and dutifully mailing them off to me. It made the Summer of separation bearable for both of us.

Kim also mailed me a shirt that Summer. It was a cotton shirt probably made in India or somewhere, white, and very cool. Long sleeved with a long v-neck. I wore the hell out of that shirt until it got too small to wear. I wouldn't put it in the dryer, but it still shrank. It was my favorite shirt ever. You couldn't find anything like that in the Midwest at the time.

No couple had ever loved each other more than her and I. Of that, I was sure.

It was Romeo and Juliet without the dying part. There's nothing like being young and in love. You can't get that back. It only happens once. If you're lucky. I was very lucky.

And as the Summer of '79 wore down, she came up with a plan for me to go visit her in Rhode Island just before the new school year would start. The anticipation was almost unbearable. That flash of lightening sometimes leaves a millisecond of glow in the clouds. That was what it was like for me that Summer. Being in that millisecond of glow and waiting for the next bolt to hit.

Chapter Four

I had heard that if you want to know what you are getting into with a bride, take a long look at her Mother. I did that. And to be perfectly honest, I could see her Mother in Kim. It didn't change my mind for a second. I would marry Kim in a heartbeat.

I was finally going to see Kim again. I was anxious and nervous and elated all at the same time. We had been planning this trip for weeks, and as I boarded the flight from St. Louis, I remember thinking, this is it. This is important. I was going to 141 Main Street, Wickford, Rhode Island. An address I was so familiar with from the dozens of letters she'd sent me. I was finally going to be there, in person, and put a real place to that street address.

I bought traveler's checks. Probably only $300. worth, but that's the sort of thing you did in 1979. You didn't carry that much cash around when you were going out of state. And it made it that much more fun anyway. I don't remember anything about the flight other than the fact that I was again, nervous as nine kinds of hell.

I had met her Dad briefly, but now I was going to be meeting her Mother, her younger brother, and aunts and uncles and God knows whom else. Would they like me? What would they be like? What did her home look like? Where would we be going? She just told me she had it all planned. So Kim was in control. Kim controlled the relationship. Kim controlled everything. I just didn't realize it at the time.

I touched down at the airport, and Kim was there to greet me. It was incredible, seeing her standing there, among a crowd of strangers. We hugged and kissed. She was incredibly excited to see me. I was still in the sky, ten thousand feet and climbing.

The first place she took me, straight from the airport, was to a fresh fish market. "Pick out anything you want and I will cook it for dinner tonight" she said. I felt woozy. The combination of the anxiety of the trip and the smell of the fish market made me feel sick, and I just couldn't do it. I told her I felt sick and I didn't want anything right now. She understood, and we went on to her parent's home.

The house was amazing. A two story historic home with massive hard wood floors that had been refinished and shined like a mirror. Her grandmother lived downstairs, but there was also a separate guest room with a full bath on the lower level. This would be where I would stay. It was actually Kim's room but she let me use it and would go upstairs to sleep on the couch at night. Kim would sneak downstairs late in the evening to be with me. Upstairs was where her brother and parents lived. And the first thing we did in that little guest room that day was made mad, passionate love. She had an amazing tan. So where she was not tanned, where her bikini had been, made for a stark contrast in skin tone. I had never seen anything like that. It made her being nude, well, accentuated. The whole experience was almost overwhelming. I could have stayed with her in that room with her for the rest of my life and been happy.

Her father was raised in that house, and his father and *his* father!

Kim's great grandfather, George Jordan, and his wife Josephine (Smith) Jordan purchased the house in August of 1900. Kim was the fourth generation of Jordans to be in that house. And she had relatives all over the area. It was built in 1795. To put it in perspective, The United States of America was only 19 years old when the house was built. Here Kim and I were, only twenty years old, making love in that very house. We were roughly the same age as The United States of America was when the house was built and there we were, together and in love in that same house. The home was 184 years old when I went there for my historic visit in 1979. It remains in the Jordan family to this day. Some 112 years as of this writing. I met her parents, and her Dad, Al Jordan, was very cool and laid back. Her Mother, Jan Jordan, on the other hand, came off as a bit cold and maybe even apprehensive about Kim's relationship with me. That was my first impression at least. And her brother, Cameron, just wasn't there at all. I was use to Moms being kind, nurturing, loving, and I am sure Kim's Mom was all of those things. Just not towards me.

She wasn't rude, but she didn't greet me with a big smile and a hug either. Life isn't a song or a movie, and sometimes can throw you a curve. I don't know what I expected, really. My Mother had welcomed Kim into our family immediately with care and respect. My Mother was great! She had raised me and my sister as a single parent. And she loved Kim. But Kim's Mother didn't know me at all. And I don't blame her for being cautious. I was a stranger from Missouri, a thousand miles away, and her daughter was young and obviously in love with me. Had it been my daughter, I would have been apprehensive too. I just didn't quite have that perspective then.

That week was one of the best weeks of my life. I couldn't have asked for a better vacation. And Kim played the role of lover, friend and tour guide. Each day, we did something new and different. At one of the small shops she took me to, I found a cool black leather bracelet with silver spiked metal studs. Totally punk rock. You couldn't find that stuff in the Midwest at the time. I bought one.

And there was the horizontal black and white striped shirt I got in the style of old pirates but came back into fashion made popular by new wave bands. We went out to eat almost every night. Including the restaurant she had worked at that Summer. I wish I could remember the name of that restaurant. It was great. I bet it is still in business.

Funny how you remember little details that may seem trivial. Yet mean so much. Kim had to do our laundry midweek and they had a washer and dryer in the big bathroom upstairs. There was a window in the bathroom, and instead of putting the wet washed clothes in the drier, Kim hoisted them outside on a clothesline in their backyard to dry in the sun.

There was a rope on pulleys, and I watched as she strung each piece of clothing on the rope with clothes pins, then pulled the rope to make room for the next garment, and so forth, until all of the clothes were stretched out on this clothes line that ran to a great tree in their backyard two stories up.

It was a smart system because it eliminated the need to carry heavy wet clothing outside to hang up to dry. I was fascinated. You could tell she had been doing it since she was a child. It was very impressive to me, but like breathing to her. She was used to that kind of work. The image of her doing that has stuck with me for all these years.

There was a drive-in movie theater we went to one night. Kim knew I loved those. I spent many weekends at the I-70 drive-in in St. Peter's, Missouri. I don't remember what movies we saw that night or even the name of the drive-in theater in R.I., but it was so much fun! There's something about being in a car with a girl at a drive-in movie. I can't think of anything more romantic. It was raining that night, which made the intimacy of being inside a car all the more appealing. This particular drive-in, you had to tune your car radio to a certain frequency to be able to hear the movie, and since it was raining a bit, we had the windshield wipers on. So at the end of the night, the battery had been worn down and the car wouldn't start! I don't remember who gave us a jump-start. But we made it home.

We had dinner with her parent's at her house one night. It was nice. And I felt like her Mom was opening up to me a bit. But there wasn't much time for her to get to know me really.

One of Kim's plans was to have her brother, Cameron, take us out on the family sailboat. He wasn't around much, though and I wasn't even sure if it would happen. I had never been on a sailboat.

Wickford harbor was beautiful. We went to some sort of affair on the docks one night with her parents. It was a great late Summer night, and I chit chatted with her Dad and a lot of other people in the community. East coast people weren't that much different than people in the Midwest, I remember thinking. They sometimes came off as a bit snooty at first, but once they opened up and got to know you, they were regular people. I am sure they were professionals who had a good deal more money than what I was used to seeing, but they were people just the same.

I fit in just fine, I thought. Kim and I hadn't gotten to the stage of where we would live if we ever got married, but I was already thinking, *I could live here and be quite happy*. That was in the back of my mind. But then again, I could have lived in a cardboard box and been happy if I was with Kim.

There was a great indoor shopping mall we went to in Providence. Shopping malls were just starting to take off at the time. The largest one in the country at the time was in fact Northwest Plaza in St. Louis, Missouri. But Kim wanted to show me hers, so we went. I was smoking a cigarette as we were getting ready to walk into the mall when Kim told me I had to put it out. "Why?" I asked. "They don't allow smoking in the mall," she said. "You've got to be kidding me!" I replied. That was the craziest damn thing I'd ever of. I don't remember anything else about that mall.

From there we went to *Mansion Row*. I don't know what it was called, but it was this street of mansions. Huge gates out front, like Elvis Presley's Graceland. I remember her taking a photo of me hanging off of one those gates. I climbed up about 10 feet, turned around, and she snapped a picture. It's a wonder I didn't get arrested. We had so much fun!

Then there was the trip to Block Island. A tiny little tourist trap of an island with all the charm of old New England you could ask for. We took the ferry there, and I got a little seasick. Once on the island, we walked around and went into the various shops. We probably had lunch somewhere, and then spent time on the beach. I had a camera, of course, and took a photo of Kim lying out on the beach in her bikini. She got genuinely pissed off about it. Kim did not like having her picture taken, ever. I never understood that. She had a figure to kill for. Kim was very insecure about her looks for some reason. She was humble in that respect, or at least that's how I saw it. So she got mad at me, but that passed in a minute. It might have been the first time I saw her mad though.

Then again, she got mad at her Mother probably a couple of days earlier. Or later. I don't remember.

I was downstairs in my guest room at her parent's house when Kim came down all upset. She explained that her Mother had questioned her about me smoking pot in their house. Now keep in mind, I didn't smoke pot at all anymore, and I certainly wouldn't have brought any with me on a plane to Rhode Island. But for some reason, I guess Kim thought I might want to, and had acquired a few joints for me just in case. Ever the all-accommodating Kim. Apparently there was a conversation between her and her Mother that escalated into an all out argument. And this is where it gets weird. According to Kim's story as I remember it, she told her Mother that no, I had not smoked any pot, but Kim produced the pre-rolled joints to her Mother and said basically, *see! Here!*

As if to say, *"But if he wanted to, he would!"* It didn't make any sense to me, and I felt bad that it happened. I was a total innocent bystander. That was between her and her Mom.

They butted heads big time. I am sure that wasn't the first time. I had heard that if you want to know what you are getting into with a bride, take a long look at her Mother. I did that. And to be perfectly honest, I could see her Mother in Kim. It didn't change my mind for a second. I would marry Kim in a heartbeat.

Her brother did take us on the sailboat, and it was great! But the kid was not a happy camper. I don't think he spoke a word the whole time. It was obvious he was doing it out of some sort of obligation. We got into a dingy, and he rowed us out to the sailboat like a hired hand. I had no clue what was going on between him and his sister. I could only guess that he was pissed off that she was using the family car all week to show me around. I think he was a couple of years younger, but he damn well knew how to sail that boat. And it was at least a 25 footer. I had bought a pair of cool black sunglasses, and wore those. Since the guy didn't talk at all, we just ignored him and enjoyed the ride.

The splashing salt water, the speed and angles the boat took, the sound of the sail and the smell of the ocean. I will never forget it. But I didn't understand what the problem was with her brother. Looking back on it, I put it down to his age. I would have liked to talk to him at least. I didn't understand the family dynamics at all. It wasn't what I was used to.

I don't remember meeting any of Kim's friends. I don't remember why. I never understood that either.

We went to some relative's house for dinner

another night. I don't remember if it was an aunt, uncle or cousin. It doesn't matter, but they were all very nice people, and we had dinner at this house. After dinner, Kim started showing me the house. It was just a regular sized house, a couple of bedrooms, etc. and then she told me the most amazing thing.

"I am going to inherit this house," she said. "My brother is going to get the boat house, but I want this house, so when we get married, we can live here."

My head was spinning off my body. *What?* I thought. I don't even remember what I said. I can't put enough explanation points behind what I was thinking. A part of me doubted that it would come to be. I probably said something like "Great. OK." She had already decided that we would get married and live happily ever after in this house. I don't even remember who the hell lived there, and when would this happen? When would she inherit this house? I may be forgetting the details. But it doesn't matter. She was sweetening the pot perhaps. The girl from Rhode Island had already won my heart. I would have lived anywhere with her. Anywhere. With her. Nothing else mattered.

I am going to say "I don't remember" a lot, but somehow, that amazing trip ended, and I don't remember if we returned to St. Louis separately or together. I would like to say we flew out together. But maybe not. She might have come a week or so later.

It's funny how you remember some things so vividly and others not at all.

It's amazing that I remember as much as I do after all these years. Imagine what I do remember times ten. Because I probably only remember ten percent, or less, of what happened.

It was time to go to school. Our first year together at Webster College. We were just starting our lives together. I'd stayed at her home in Wickford, met her parents and brother, and other family.

So we went from 141 Main Street, Wickford,

Rhode Island to

470 East Lockwood Avenue, Webster Groves, Missouri.

This story was just beginning …

Chapter Five

I was a drummer and she was dancer. It was perfect. We were supposed to be together. That's just how it was.

She loved peanut M&M's. And Blue Nun wine. I loved everything about her. The way she walked. I could tell it was her coming down the hallway. I could tell by her steps. The pace, the very sound. My favorite pair of shoes she had were clogs. It was a very distinctive sound. Like a fingerprint. I loved the way that she talked, laughed and cried. I loved the way that she blinked her eyes and crinkled up her face when she was thinking. I loved watching her sleep. I loved the way that she breathed. The feel and sound of her breathe as she lay sleeping next to me. I had never loved anyone like that.

I only took three classes that first semester at Webster College. I don't remember why, but it may have been because I was planning on continuing to work at Hussmann. Somewhere along the line, I decided that wouldn't be a good idea. I would never get to see Kim, except on weekends, if I'd have kept working. I wanted to see her every day.

So I had some free time that first semester. I rented a room in a huge house in Webster Groves not far from the school. I think it was $15. a week. And it was a big room. But I spent most of my time in Kim's dorm. I only went to the rented room to sleep. And it wasn't long before I ended up moving in with her. The lady I rented the room from was nuts. She ran an answering service from home, and her desk was at the bottom of the stairs, where I had to go to get up to my room on the second floor. Well, she wasn't actually crazy, she was just a talker. Every time I came in, she would stop and ask me a million questions. "How is school? How is Kim? What are you doing tonight?" It went on and on. Ten or fifteen minutes at least. I just wanted to come and go as I pleased, but it wasn't like that at all. So I ended up staying with Kim in her dorm. I was there most of the time anyway. That became home for Kim and I.

They broke ground on Loretto Hall on November 1st, 1927. Thirty-one years to the day before I was born. I didn't know that we shared a birthday at the time. But I knew it was a magical building for me.

Loretto Hall, a castle worthy of a princess and a prince. We reigned together quietly from the third floor.

It was a magnificent four story structure. It looked like a castle. And it had not changed a bit in its 52 years when Kim and I lived there. It was a tiny room. Probably about 10 feet by six, if that. Long and narrow. It had a twin bed, dresser and student desk. A window at the end where the desk sat overlooked the parking lot three floors down. That was it. I could see my car parked in the parking lot from that window. There was a small clothes closet and an even smaller one next to that which housed a small sink and medicine cabinet. We bought a little dorm refrigerator from J.C. Penney. I opened up a charge account at the store to do that. This would be our home, and for the most part, it was all we needed. I would have lived there forever with her. She bought a rug for the floor next to the bed, otherwise it was all hardwood floors. I loved that room. Or loved being there with her. Because I wasn't supposed to be there, I had to kind of hide out. There was an elevator right next to her door that went down to the lobby. That is probably why her room was so small. The other rooms were much bigger. But when they put in the elevator, I guess they cut that room in half. There was no security, so it was pretty easy for me to come and go without being noticed. And I was an actual student, so everyone knew me anyway. I had to get up real early and sneak down the hall to the shower room before anyone else did. Then I could slip into the elevator next to our room and go downstairs to the lobby to go to classes. The dorm was connected to the main building, so I didn't even have to go outside. It was a very insulated environment, warm and cozy despite its size.

One night while we were snuggling in bed and watching TV there was a knock at the door. It was the kid from across the hall. I had to hide in the closet while she talked to him. She didn't invite him in of course, but the kid just kept talking and talking about nothing. I came very close to leaping out of the closet and beating the shit out of him. He finally left but that was the longest five minutes of my life. Otherwise, we stayed in her room together in the evenings and weren't bothered by anyone. We would be doing homework, talking, playing music or watching TV. She wanted me to be there. I think it was even her idea for me to stay there and stop paying the crazy lady the $15. a week.

Somehow, it just happened. I wouldn't have been there without her blessing, that's for sure.

On most weekends, we would go home to my parent's house in O'Fallon, near St. Charles. It was kind of out in the country. A twenty-five minute drive down Highway 40 West to Highway K. There was nothing on the few miles of Highway K except for farmland. And a convenience store called The K Shop. But it was nice to get off campus. She had no place else to go. By then, she was already a part of my family. We'd been a couple for six months or more, and my family was crazy about her. My niece Billie was nine years old, and she adored Kim. She was constantly seeking Kim's attention. When we would visit my sister's house, even as we were leaving, Billie would be following us. "Kim! Look!!" she would yell, as she turned cartwheels in the front yard. Billie would be forever influenced by Kim. She went on to study dance because of Kim. I had by then moved my old upright piano into my sister's house. To my dismay, they had painted it black.

Kim got real sick one time, with allergies, and actually had to be hospitalized. I was worried as hell. She was only there a couple of days, but it was very scary. I took her to the hospital and was there most of the time. I think my Mother and Sister also came to see her. I thought, "this girl has no family here. I am her family." I wanted to take care of her, and did. I hated seeing her sick. But they gave her IV treatments and soon she was fine. She might as well have been on her deathbed as far as I was concerned. Even though it wasn't a serious illness, it made me realize what true love and commitment was about. It meant having each other's backs, no matter what. She had been there for me during the stupid "drug bust," and I was there for her when she was sick. The idea of supporting the one you love in any time of need is the fundamental basis of that love. You have to be an umbrella. That's what it is all about. Stick together and stay together no matter what. That is what sustains a relationship. There was no doubt in my mind that we would be together forever, no matter what. There's something magical and empowering about that. I was a drummer and she was dancer. It was perfect. We were supposed to be together. That's just how it was. And I had every reason by then to believe in magic.

It's sometimes the little moments I remember. One time she hurried into our room between classes to get something, and I was there, and she literally only had seconds. I went to kiss her as she was rushing out of the room and she darted her tongue in my mouth. It was quick and unexpected. Nonverbal communication. I'll never forget that one second.

We did do some socializing together at school of course. There were organized parties we'd attend. It was obvious from the start to all of the students that we were boyfriend/girlfriend. I distinctly remember people telling us that we made a great looking couple. We both had long, blonde hair. We both bleached our hair to look that way, mine slightly less blonde than hers. I would color her hair for her every couple of months. And she would use a curling iron to curl her hair around her beautiful face. It was the Seventies. I was very short, about 5'5" but she was a few inches shorter, maybe 5'2". We had photos taken at a professional photo studio in St. Louis called Olan Mills.

I don't remember whose idea that was, but they turned out great. I doubt that it was Kim's idea, since she loathed having pictures taken at the time. It might have been my Mother's idea, because I doubt that I would have had the foresight to do it.

We hooked up with our friends Jim and Pat a couple of times. One weekend, they came to my parent's house. I think it was for my birthday. Kim made lasagna. They were over an hour late getting there for dinner, which kind of pissed us off. Jim had been trying to finish up a last minute present for me. A fish aquarium. So that made them being late a little easier to take. But we kind of drifted away from them. They had a lot of drama going on and we just weren't into that.

Kim and I took a walk one evening at my parent's place and ran into Jeannie Ickenbach. She was a neighbor and a friend. She was sort of my girlfriend before Kim. I say sort of because she was only 14 when I met her. So nothing much happened, we just hung out together, and I did care about her, but it wasn't really a serious relationship. She must have been 15 or so when we ran into her while taking a walk. She was at least six months pregnant at the time. Jeannie walked with us and talked a blue streak. Kim wasn't real thrilled about that and when we went back inside she told me how stupid she thought Jeannie was, messing up her life by getting pregnant at such an early age. Kim was right, but I just said, "Yeah, but she's just a kid. She didn't know what she was doing." Kim had a different opinion. I could understand and even sympathize with Jeannie. Kim was having none of it. It was black and white. Jeannie allowed herself to be taken advantage of. We didn't talk about her after that. The piano songs **"Mirror of Mistakes," "Before I Fall,"** and **"Most Of My Money,"** had all been inspired in part by my very strange and short lived relationship with Jeannie Ickenbach. As well as the acoustic guitar song **"A Lover And A Friend."** Of course, I never told Kim that. I am not even sure if I ever played her those recordings. I know I played them on the piano for her. So she knew the songs.

Kim was taking mostly dance classes, and I was taking writing. I worked on the weekly student newspaper, and continued writing poetry/lyrics. We had our school friends apart from each other. She hung out with some of the other dance majors, and I started exploring the local new wave music scene. It was a different world.

I would occasionally go see local bands, and quickly became friends with some of them. One was called **The Retros**. Bob, the bass player, also went to Webster. And there was **Cool Jerk, The Ooz Kicks, The Clones, The Felons**, and **The Welders**, an all girl group. Rusty, the guitarist for **The Welders**, also went to school at Webster. It was a small scene, and I was quick to get to know people. I don't think Kim ever went with me to any of the concerts. It just wasn't quite her cup of tea. So we did do some things apart. But we were secure enough with each other not to let that bother us.

We were making tentative plans together along the way. We would get married, she said, after the following school year. The wedding would take place in Rhode Island. Her parents wouldn't have it any other way, she said. We were dreaming of our life together. We would go to college after that at Penn State, her to graduate school and me to finish undergrad. I would have gone anywhere, but it was important to me to have some kind of plan.

We would buy an electric car, she said. "Ok, where

will we plug it in at?" I asked. "We'll run an extension cord," she said. Of course! I pictured us living on the third floor of a dorm, with a long extension cord running out of our window down to our electric car in the parking lot.

It would be great! She told me they had special little apartments for married students, with eat in kitchens and everything! "But I don't want to have any babies" she explained. I didn't even question that, but I might have said something like "You don't want any children?" "Well, we could adopt a five year old. Maybe a little black boy," she replied. I didn't even question it.

She wanted to have her own dance school. That was the plan. And I would do lights and sound. I promised her I would do that. It seemed like a great plan. I would have her back, I would support her in any way I could. And she talked about having a prenuptial agreement. I sort of knew what that was and told her I was against it. It seemed liked a negative thing to me. You don't go into a marriage making plans for it to end, I thought. Forever is forever. It boggled my mind. I don't know where she was coming from with that. But it certainly seemed like we were going to get married.

In October we went to a pumpkin farm with my family. The only reason I remember that is because I have pictures. We sat on a huge pumpkin and Kim very reluctantly smiled for the camera. Kim hated taking pictures.

I turned 21 that year. I was born on November 1st, 1958. The day after Halloween. We went to the college Halloween party and danced. I want to say Kim wore a toga, or a bed sheet made to look like a toga. But that could have been another party. A couple of the kids from **The Ooz Kicks** were there, and other friends. Some people were in costume. There were a lot of theater majors at Webster. When we went back to her room, there was a surprise waiting for me. Kim had snuck away from the party and decorated our dorm room for my birthday. Steamers, maybe some balloons, I don't remember now. But it was very touching. She probably had a card and a gift for me. But what I remember most was her decorating the room in honor of my 21st birthday. You only turn 21 once. And I couldn't have been in a happier place. I will never forget that.

The steps at Loretto Hall. I don't remember there being so many. There were fourteen steps. It seemed like two at the time.

On a weekend at my parent's house we were watching the news and they announced that President Reagan was starting up the draft. I was eligible. "There's no way they are going to take my Steven!" she said. My parents were in the room at the time and heard this as well. "We will move to Canada before I let that happen!" she said. And we believed her. That's how committed Kim was. There was no doubt in my mind that we would get married and live together forever. Even if it meant in Canada.

Shortly after, I did a feature story on **The Retros** for the school paper. Bob the bass player told me they were looking to replace their drummer and asked me if I'd be interested. "Hell yes!" I said. **The Retros** were the coolest band in St. Louis at the time. They were kind of like **The Ramones**, jeans and black leather jackets. In fact, they had opened for **The Ramones** in St. Louis the year before. Kim was very encouraging. She even drew a little picture of four mop tops and wrote **"The Retros!"** on it and pinned it up in our room for me. So off I went to rehearse with them one night, and everything went great! I was very excited and Kim was happy for me. But not more than a couple of weeks later, I ran into Bob at school and he said "Oh Steve, **The Retros** suck!" "What do you mean?" I asked. "They decided not to kick him out of the band. It sucks," he replied. And just like that, I was out of **The Retros.**

We went to my Aunt Cona's house just before Christmas break. Aunt Cona was my Mother's older sister and had been a very successful beauty shop owner. Cona adored Kim, and we had a very nice family Christmas together. I remember thinking how they were similar because they were both strong willed women. My Uncle Lonnie was there too. And he whispered to me what a catch Kim was because she was so attractive. That was the difference between Lonnie and Cona.

Winter break came, and Kim had to go home to Rhode Island for a couple of weeks. We were sad, but it would be short lived. While she was gone, I went to a New Wave club and met a girl. I'd seen her around before, and she was very good looking and kind of liked me. We ended up going to my car and making out. I suddenly realized what I was doing was wrong and stopped. I felt real guilty. What the hell was I thinking? I wasn't. That was the problem. I made a promise to myself then and there that I would never do that again. And when I picked Kim up from the airport the following week, I probably hugged her a little more tightly. If we were going to get married, I couldn't let a really cute girl who liked me come between us. I would never cheat again. We saw that same girl at that same club awhile later, on one of the rare occasions that Kim went along with me to a new wave club. And the girl kept staring at us, even as we were all leaving. "Who is that?" Kim asked me. "Just some girl" I said.

Rusty of **The Welders** asked me one day if I would consider being their drummer. "Yeah, sure" I said. So I told Kim and she was not so supportive this time. I guess the idea of me hanging out with a group of attractive female musicians didn't sit well with her. But I went with Rusty to a rehearsal one night anyway. As I recall, I just explained to Kim that it was only rock and roll music. They just happened to be girls, that's all. I don't remember what I told her really. But the "audition" went really well. I didn't know their songs, but I could play drums and just kept up with them. It was rock and roll. I could do that. After we played music in the basement, we sat around the kitchen table and talked about music, their plans for the band and so forth. They were huge **Beatle's** fans too. Two of the girls were sisters, half-Japanese. They were cool as hell. And they explained to me that maybe having a guy in the band would make them seem a little more credible or serious or something. I told them that I would do it, but I was a little apprehensive that by being in the band I would take away from their all girl persona. I was afraid I wouldn't be accepted by their following. But I wanted to be in a band and I liked them and they liked me. So I was in the band. They gave me a cassette of their four-song demo they'd recorded in an actual studio so I could learn the songs. I took the tape and went back home to 470 East Lockwood Ave.

Kim and I both worked part-time through the work-student program tutoring English to foreign exchange students. She had befriended the older lady who was the secretary of that department. As I was walking into the office to turn in my time sheet I overheard Kim complaining to the lady about me playing music with **The Welders**. I had only had one rehearsal with them up to that point. It was probably the same week of me going to **The**

Welders audition. I don't remember her exact words, but she was bitching about it. And as I turned the corner, Kim saw me and realized I must have heard her. Again, her eyes showed everything. Apparently, this was a huge deal to Kim. I just turned my timesheet in and pretended like I didn't hear anything.

The following weekend we were at my parent's house. They had a finished basement with a family room and bed, etc. which is where we spent a lot of our time. I had a cassette player, the Sony, and went to put in **The Welders** tape and listen to it with headphones. The first song started. . ."While I was making my social debut. I was accosted and held up by you." Then "Ding dong the wicked witch is dead!" What the hell?

Kim had recorded over the tape with some rendition of **"The Wicked Witch Is Dead"** from **"The Wizard Of Oz!"** She explained that she was working on choreographing a dance for a class and that it was an accident, she thought it was a blank tape. I was visibly pissed off. To this day, I don't know if she did it on purpose or if it was an accident.

The year swept by quickly. I had applied for my own dorm room for the following year, figuring even if I stayed in Kim's room, it would look better and I wouldn't have to sneak around. She had applied to be an R. A. (Resident Assistant) but she didn't get it. Had she gotten the position, it would have meant either a free room or really reduced rate. She told someone, I don't remember who, in front of me, that she didn't get the position because of me. Although true, it still hurt my feelings.

Events run together, but at some point, Kim told me that maybe we should go to school at George Washington University, or somewhere. I don't know why now, but I told her she had to get the plan together. She seemed to be changing her mind. I kind of flew off the handle a bit I think. I didn't like the idea of not knowing what we were going to be doing or where we were going to go. I would go anywhere, just don't keep changing plans on me. She just wasn't sure, and I don't know if that had to do with money and scholarships or what. She was a straight A student, I know that. Straight A's all the time. She was super ambitious and a very hard worker. I would type her papers for her on my electric Smith-Corona typewriter in our room. This was before personal computers. And I would have to edit for spelling and grammar. But this girl was smart as hell and on top of it when it came to schoolwork. I was always more than happy to help her in any way I could, but much of her work was physical. She was a dance major!

One of our nightly rituals became me giving her a back rub. What she did was incredibly physical. And she taught me how to give her a back rub. I think sometimes I did a great job. I was very serious about it. Sometimes, when I was free and I knew she had a dance class, I would go watch her for a few minutes. She couldn't see me, but I would watch her dance, and I don't remember if I ever mentioned it to her. One class in particular that I observed was "African Dance." I think she was the only white girl in the class, and she would tell me how hard it was. So I went to observe, and it was incredible. The instructor seemed to be hard on her, but guess what? She aced that class too.

It had been a long, short year. Like dog years again. I had written a lot, including poems for and about Kim. This is the one I remember the best. I am still proud of it for its honest simplicity:

Sleep Sweet

Close your pretty eyes

Relax your weary mind
Lay down on the bed

And I'll sooth your aching muscles

Sleep sweet

Sleep sweet

Listen to this lullaby

And I'll love you in the morning

I'll love you till I die

The school year ended and it was time once again for her to go home for the Summer. But somehow it wasn't as bad as the first time. We had a good year, I thought. A few bumps, but nothing any couple can't get through together. I felt more secure in our relationship, and we were still happy and in love. I was a drummer and she was dancer. It was perfect. We were supposed to be together. That's just how it was.

Kim left a few boxes of winter clothes with me and her birth control pills. I took her to the airport, and this time, I don't even think she cried. I had already told **The Welders** I would not be in the band, and had very few plans for the Summer. Kim worked as always, and I went to the drive-in on weekends by myself. It was a very uneventful Summer. But that would change dramatically on the first day of the 1980-81 school year.

One of the stone figures on Webster Hall. I didn't think about them then, but there they were. This one seems to be in pain. The irony of that didn't hit me until I took this photograph.

Chapter Six

Someone once said "Love is giving someone the ability to destroy you, and hoping that they won't."

The only phone call I remember getting from Kim that Summer would come back to haunt me later.

I said the Summer of 1980 was uneventful. And it was. There weren't the daily letters from Kim. I wasn't socializing much. I don't remember what I did other than once again writing and recording songs. I made an attempt at it, but it was not that great. For some reason, I just wasn't that inspired. They say when you become comfortable and happy, you lose that hunger, that motivation, that drive! Kim and I were a couple, and I didn't feel that desperate need to win the girl. I became complacent I guess. But there's something to be said about being comfortable, confident and happy in a relationship. It just doesn't always make for good art. Paul McCartney probably suffered from that. So there were no letters and very few phone calls from Kim. In fact, most of the time when I would call her, I talked to her Mother, and Kim was always out. The only song I remember writing for the tape I sent her that Summer kind of sums it up.

It was called **"Nothing Valid."** Believe it or not, the actual music or melody to that song was pretty good. The rest of the tape, I don't remember. But I am sure there were a couple of good ones in there. But **"Nothing Valid"** was uninspiring yet captured the moment.

My parents and Aunt Cona and Uncle Wayne went on a road trip that Summer and made arrangements to go to Wickford, R.I. to meet Kim and her parents. It wasn't the sole purpose of the trip, but a side stop because they were going to be in the area. I thought that was cool. They arrived at the old house on Main Street and Kim was there to greet them but her parents were at work. Kim worked at night as a waitress. They talked to Kim awhile and she told them to drive down highway One and where to go to check out the Rhode Island sights. Later that evening, they went back to Kim's house and met Al and Jan Jordan. They had dinner with them in their home. Then the Jordan's took them out on their sailboat, just as Brother Cameron had done for me the Summer before. According to my Mother, the Jordan's were very nice to them and they all had a good time. They went back to the Jordan house and got to see Kim for a few more minutes after she got off work. My Mother said that the sailboat ride was great. I was glad our parent's got to meet and seemed to enjoy each other's company.

The only phone call I remember getting from Kim that Summer would come back to haunt me later. And I don't remember when it happened really. I don't know if it was one month before she was to return to St. Louis or more than that. Long distance calls cost money so we didn't talk much ever. All I remember about the conversation was her asking me to mail her birth control pills to her. "So I can be ready when I get back there" she said. I didn't think much about it really. I guess it made sense. Apparently you have to take the pill a week or so before it starts working. Kim had everything planned. So I complied. I found and mailed her birth control pills. It was just like Kim to always be thinking ahead.

Finally it was time for school to start again, but this time, it would be different. I had my own dorm room in Loretto Hall. Kim had gotten a bigger room, and things were going to be great!

I spotted Kim walking down the hall in the airport coming off the plane towards me, finally, again. We hugged. But something was wrong. I damn well knew Kim, and something wasn't right. The hug wasn't right. On the drive from the airport to the college, she didn't say much, but I knew something was going on. I just didn't know what. We took her luggage to her new dorm room in Loretto Hall and she said she wanted to go get something to eat. So we walked across the street from Webster to this little sandwich shop. We sat down to eat and she finally started talking. She said she didn't really know what her plans were going to be, but that they would not be including me. I don't remember what she said. It just took a few seconds. She told me in a public place. She had it planned. I didn't know what to say. So these words came out of my mouth out of nowhere, "It's cool." I said. I don't know where that came from. Just as my words "I will always love you, I will never leave you" had come before. I guess it was the quickest way of saying "I get it, stop, I don't need to hear anymore." She started talking again, and I just held my hand up to stop her and repeated, "No, it's cool." I stood up and walked out of the restaurant.

But it was anything but cool. It was the opposite of cool. I couldn't handle it. My whole world had just blown up and ended. It was like an out of body experience that remains with me to this very day. I just said "it's cool" because I couldn't deal with it and it was the first thing that popped into my head. Those words were somehow channeled through me. I was speaking in tongues. I was totally devastated. And I had no idea what I was going to do. Something happened over the Summer with Kim Jordan and to this day, I can't quite figure it out. Only Kim knows that.

I walked out of that restaurant like a zombie. My life was changed in seconds, and I had no time to prepare for it. "What am I going to do now?" I thought.

I don't know how I managed to get across the street, let alone through the rest of that semester. I walked blindly back to 470 East Lockwood Ave. but it was no longer our home. She had those Winter clothes at my sister's house so she asked me if we could go get them. My Mother was there, and everyone acted like nothing was going on. My sister chit chatted with Kim as if nothing had changed. But everything had. My Mother made some excuse to leave the house with me, and she drove me around the block. She asked me what I was going to do. "I don't know!" I sobbed. I held my head in my hands and cried like a baby. She basically told me I had to get it together and figure it out. Everything I knew to be true was crashing around me. I can't imagine how difficult that had to be for my Mother to see. We went back inside, and again pretended like nothing was going on. Kim and I collected her belongings and drove back to Webster.

She gave me back some stuff she had of mine, including the **"boyfriend"** package. That hurt like hell. Her handing that heart shaped box back was so symbolic to me. But I don't think she meant it that way. I think she just realized that I should have it. But I wished she would have asked to keep it. Kim wasn't into holding onto anything though. Let it go and move on. She was in a different position than I was. I am sure she had no idea that giving me that package back killed me inside. One thing that she did not offer to return was the promise ring. And I thought about that for a week or so, nonstop. I finally concluded that I should ask for it back. That was not at all an easy task. I remember we were in her big new dorm room, and I just came right out and asked her if I could have the ring back, please. She didn't hesitate, but for some reason, I still felt the unnecessary need to justify my request by explaining that it had been my grandmother's ring. It's possible that she didn't want to go through the experience of voluntarily giving me the ring back, knowing how symbolic that is, and maybe she was just putting it off. I don't know. In retrospect, I should have let her keep it. My soundtrack during the break-up semester became Elvis Costello's album **"Get Happy!"** It was as if he had written it with me in mind. Oddly enough, the Costello album we danced to the night of the "I will always love you, I will never leave you" party was called **"This Year's Model."** And for some reason, the song I remember us dancing to that night was called **"Lip Service."** I could only shake my head in disbelief, and cry.

Having coffee one morning at my mother's house shortly after the Kim break-up, 1980. The eyes tell everything.

Like a shooting star. It was gone. But unlike a pretty flash in the sky, this was my life and my love. So the defense mechanisms kicked in. I honestly don't know how I survived. But the first thing I did was move the hell out of Loretto Hall. I had a friend from the year before named Scott Katz. The first time I met Scott, he had a **Sex Pistols** T-shirt on. He was from Houston, Texas, and had a big time corporate lawyer Uncle in St. Louis. We got an apartment together. Scott was a bad influence, yet a necessary one at the time. He was a spoiled little rich kid, I thought. But he was there when I needed something. Had it not been for him, I probably wouldn't have stayed in school that semester.

On Spring break, Scott and I drove down to New Orleans and stayed in a frat house at Tulane University. Some high school friend of his went there. We went down to Bourbon Street and hit all the bars, of course. It was a crazy time. I met one of the college girls while we were partying on Bourbon Street and we hit it off pretty well. She was quite attractive, a skinny brunette, and I ended up walking her home to her dorm that night, and kissed her goodnight. I would never see that girl again. For the first time in awhile, I had a good time and kissed a girl. *I am still alive*, I thought. It was a big ego booster for me. If I knew how to get hold of her, I would thank that girl right now. Of course, she would think I was crazy, but that's okay. I really believe in karma and doing what is right. That's a big deal for me.

Another road trip Scott and I took was all the way to his hometown of Houston, TX. We stayed at his Mother's condo, and it was very nice. He took me to an Oiler's football game. He was not a great friend though. He also took me to some strip club. He always thought of himself first. And I had no direction. Without Kim, I was just running wild. I managed to stay in school and took a part-time job along with Scott as a busboy at a seafood restaurant called Nantucket's Cove. And I was still seeing Kim. In fact, sometimes we did things together. I am certain Kim still cared about me, even loved me on some level. And I immediately, of course, started trying to figure out why she broke up with me. It didn't make any sense to me, so I quickly blamed her Mother. She didn't like me or the idea of her daughter getting married to anyone out of state, or before she got her Master's degree. I made it up in my head that her Mother had gotten to her over the Summer. Certainly something major happened that Summer. Maybe her parents told her that they would not help pay for her graduate school if she got married. It couldn't have been Kim's idea to break up with me, I thought. My God, that was unbelievable to think. At some point soon thereafter, I wrote a letter to Jan Jordan. I am sure it was a pitiful letter, but I don't remember what all I said. But I wanted to let her Mother know how much I loved Kim and how absolutely devastated I was that she had broken up with me. I was a mess, and I am sure that was obvious. I was looking for sympathy, I guess. To my surprise, she wrote me back right away. It was a very nice letter. She told me, basically, that time heals all wounds. It was a handwritten letter. And it made it harder to blame her Mother.

I was sort of on autopilot I guess. I didn't know what to do. I was hoping she would come out of her coma and come around to me again. It was a very strange and difficult time. I would see Kim, but it wasn't the same. It wasn't right. We were supposed to be together, but we weren't. How do you go from "I will always love you, I will never leave you," to let's have lunch? It's just not possible. Yet I tried.

Looking back on it now, it is amazing that Kim made such an effort to still be friends. She went out of her way to see me. One night her and a girlfriend came to have dinner at Nantucket's Cove because I worked there.

We went to Scott's Uncle's house together one night. They had an outside hot tub. It was me and Kim, Scott and another girl. And we were just enjoying being in the hot tub and talking. Somehow David Letterman came up. I remember her saying she did not like David Letterman. I loved Letterman at the time. Funny how you remember little things like that.

And I remember taking her out to dinner a couple of times. In a strange way, things were the same. She would order a house salad and I would order steak, then she would eat a couple of bites of my steak. "Good Lord," I said, "just order a steak!" For a couple who had broken up, it seemed we saw an awful lot of each other. One of those dinners was a double date with Scott and some girl he had been seeing. I warned Kim that, "this girl and Scott are a little immature," and after dinner, while I was driving her home, she brought that up again and totally agreed with me.

I don't know how I managed going out with her and not going home with her at the end of the night. In fact, I wasn't dealing with it very well at all, *it was killing me*. It was strange, I thought, that we would be going out at all. She knew I loved her, more than anyone ever. And I knew she loved me. I still didn't get why we weren't together. And it got to me over the Semester. Seeing her was good and bad at the same time. We were supposed to be together, I thought. It kept coming back to that. *We are supposed to be together.*

She even spent the night at my apartment one time. I don't know why that happened. We didn't make love, of course, but she stayed the night and slept in my bed. That would be the last time that would ever happen.

A staircase in Webster Hall. I hadn't touched that handrail in 33 years.

There was a knock at my apartment door one morning. It was the Maplewood police, and they asked if I was Steven Thomas. "Yes I am" I said. "Please step outside Mr. Thomas," they said. "We have an outstanding warrant for you from St. Charles County," they informed me. WHAT? So I was handcuffed and hauled off to jail. I asked what it was for, and they said possession of marijuana. WHAT?

I explained that there must be some kind of mistake, and that was already resolved more than a year ago. They said there was a police car in route to take me back to St. Charles jail. "Oh hell no!" I said. But they did let me make a phone call, and I think, once again, I called my sister. She couldn't reach my attorney, so she called our Mother, who made a quick call to St. Charles police, and said "That boy better not make it to your jail or there will be hell to pay!" They immediately radioed the police car and let me out of Maplewood jail. Apparently that warrant was never taken out of the system. It was crazy. *Just another case of bad luck*, I thought.

One night I got the bright idea of trying to stay the night in Kim's room. The idea was to sleep in the same bed with her again and maybe she would realize she still loved me and everything would go back to the way it had been. A dumb idea but I was desperate and had nothing else to go for. So I showed up at her room and told her I had gotten locked out of my apartment or something and had no place else to sleep. She was very reluctant, but allowed me to sleep with her in her bed. I tried to get a little too close to her and she wasn't having it and got very upset. "I am sorry, I will sleep on the floor!" I pleaded. But she was mad and jumped out of bed and took me downstairs to the lobby and a couch. But she brought me a pillow and a blanket. The next morning I was awakened by one of the ladies who worked there coming into the little side room I was in. But she quickly exited and left me alone. Everyone knew who I was. This was my home.

A few days later, Scott and I were at the new wave club, and he came rushing up to me screaming, "John Lennon is dead!" "What?" I said. "What are you talking about?" It was crazy. I used the pay phone to call the **St. Louis Post-Dispatch**, and after about ten minutes, finally got through to them. They confirmed it. John Lennon had been shot and killed outside the Dakota in New York City. My life would never be the same again. I wrote Kim a note. "I lost you and John Lennon in the same year."

I couldn't take it anymore. I was losing it. I knew I had to do something, and it was obvious our relationship was over. My Mother's words came rushing back to me. *"What are you going to do?"* I finished out the semester and transferred to Lindenwood College, where it had all began.

Chapter Seven

My whole Lindenwood College days never led to a serious relationship. I think that was partly because I was a little worried about getting into one after what had happened with Kim. And I just never met anyone that shook me.

I wrote Kim a letter and gave it to her just before she was to go home for Christmas break of 1980. It was just a week or so after Lennon had been killed. I wrote on the envelope not to open it until she was on the plane, but I doubt that she bothered to follow those instructions. It didn't really matter. That was just me being dramatic. I explained to her how I was transferring to Lindenwood College and that I wouldn't be around anymore. This was it. It was the most difficult and important letter that I had ever written. And it was full of emotion and honesty. I told her that she was an amazing woman at age 21 and that I could only imagine what an even more amazing woman she would be at age 40. That's how old John was when he was senselessly murdered that year. I was projecting that far into the future. And I told her that I loved her and wished I could know her and be with her when we were both 40 and beyond.

I didn't know who would be picking her up from the airport when she came back from Christmas break. It would not be me. I didn't know whom she would end up marrying and spending her life with, but I knew it would not be me. I couldn't go on another semester, another day, the way I was. Like John Lennon, I was dying. But mine was from a broken heart. I had to save myself.

Six years later, I would come face to face with Kim again.

Lindenwood surprised me. Mostly because there were no ghosts of Kim there, even though that is where our relationship began. It was such a relief! I was starting over. John Lennon's last album had a single that was being played at the time, just before his death. It was called **"Just Like Starting Over."** And that wasn't easy. I felt like a survivor. I am sure that if I had sought professional help, I would have been diagnosed with depression, and God knows what else. But I jumped into going to a different school with gusto and everything changed for me.

Oddly enough, I found myself taking a dance class at Lindenwood. It was to fulfill my physical education requirement. I had to buy dance tights, etc. I even got leg warmers. All black, of course. So here I was, taking a dance class in the very same dance studio that Kim had taken classes. Yet I didn't think about Kim. At least not consciously. I had grown to appreciate dance because of Kim, but when I was doing it, I didn't think about her. It was in the far back recesses of my mind I guess. And dance class was fun. There were only about eight of us, and only two of us were guys. The other guy was a basketball major, a black guy, and he explained to me that he was doing it for the stretching exercises. We would do stretching for half of the class. I got to where I could put one of my legs behind my head. I worked out on the parallel bars. Someone took black and white photos of me working out on the parallel bars in my black dance tights. I was finally learning the fundamentals of what it took to be a dancer. And I had to choreograph a dance for the end of the year dance concert. Just like Kim and Pat had done. Over the next couple of years, I would end up taking 3 dance classes. I made new friends and met new girls. None of them panned out for me, but I didn't care.

I think I wasn't ready to get into another relationship yet. It took a couple of years for my confidence to build up again to even think about that. But I still wrote lyrics. One was called **"The Trouble With Love."** That poem came about from me leaving a note on a girl's door. I wanted to go out with her. So I left a note on her dorm room door. It was about the awkwardness of asking for that first date. And maybe regretting leaving that note on the door.

STEVEN M THOMAS

At the end of the semester, I did think about Kim again. I knew she would be graduating from Webster, and I thought about going to her graduation. I knew her parent's would be flying in for that. And I really wanted to be there. But it was just a fleeting thought because I also knew that it would be too much for me. She would have appreciated me being there, I am sure. I just couldn't do it.

I got a job as a waiter at The Harley Hotel in Earth City, and that's when I met a girl who also worked there as a hostess named Chris Merry. She was 19 and a skinny brunette. I ended up having an affair with her, of sorts. I say affair because she actually had a boyfriend. We spent a lot of evenings together though, after work. I had an apartment on First Capitol Drive in St. Charles, and sometimes we went to my place, other times we went to Lindenwood by the old water tower. I would pitch a blanket on the grass and we would make love outside in the dark. It was wonderful. I was falling for Chris.

My roommate, David Bochman also worked at hotel, and we both had to work New Year's Eve of 1982. So we had a party at our apartment a weekend later called the ***"Did you get fucked by having to work New Year's Eve Party, Party."*** We made up fliers that that actually said that, inviting people to come. Some people from work came, including Chris, and our boss, Ed. Chris ended up sitting on my lap, and we were being pretty physical, and Ed,was kind of surprised. He had no idea that we were seeing each other outside of work. And he just said, "As long as it doesn't interfere with work, I don't care," or something like that. Chris was the first girl I'd been with since Kim. But there was no indication that she would be leaving her boyfriend for me, so I knew I had to end it. I did that in one quick swoop. I quit my job at the Harley Hotel. I explained to Chris that I was getting a job through college and that we wouldn't be seeing each other anymore. It was just that simple. It pained me though. I would talk to her on the phone ten years later when curiosity had finally gotten the better of me. She was the first girl I had been with since Kim.

The old water tower behind Lindenwood College. I took my first girlfriend after Kim, Chris, to the old water tower several times late at night after we got off work. We would bring a blanket and make love outside beneath the tower.

Sometimes my friend Mark Snow would come over to the apartment and we would play music. He had a four-track cassette recorder and brought it over along with his guitar. I had my electric guitar and a pair of bongos. The same wooden bongos my Aunt Cona had gotten me in Mexico. The same set I had used with my friend Zachary when we were six years old. We were kind of serious about doing a good job of recording. We did **"Two Of Us"** by The Beatles, which turned out surprisingly good.

We both played guitar and sang together. And we did **"Maybe Baby"** by Buddy Holly. Which was okay. And a song I'd written called **"Call Me Back."** That song was about Kim, of course. And you can imagine, with a title like that, how it went. The best way I can describe my guitar playing on that is like John Lennon's on **"Julia"** from **The White Album**. And it was dark and a bit macabre. We worked on that song for several hours and got it down probably as good as it was going to get with our limited skills. Mark thought enough of the composition to work on it with me, so I knew it had to be good. I respected his opinion. Outside of him, very few people heard that song. This was personal art for art's sake. Later, we would move our makeshift recording studio into the upstairs floor of Lindenwood's radio station KCLC. There we recorded another song I wrote called **"I Know A Song."** That I wrote for Chris Merry. With some memories of Kim thrown in.

I was working at the radio station at Lindenwood by then and had a key to the building. Mark liked **"I Know A Song"**, and we wanted to record it. I played acoustic guitar and sang and he played electric guitar on track one. I played drums and he played bass on track two.

That second year at Lindenwood, I got a dorm room in Parker Hall. I wanted to experience that again. Living in a dorm. But it was an all-male dorm, and I felt totally disconnected with most of the kids that lived there. I was a couple of years older than most of them and we had very little in common. But it was okay. Just not quite what I was hoping for. The kids at Webster were cooler. It was a performing arts school and there was the whole new wave music thing going on. I don't know what I was expecting, really. It didn't hit me right away that Kim had transferred from Lindenwood to Webster for a reason. I did it backwards. My Mother came by every Friday and slipped a twenty-dollar bill under my door, like clockwork.

Parker Hall, where I lived at Lindenwood after Kim and I broke up. I felt disconnected from the guys in the all-male dorm. After I'd live with Kim, it felt like a step backwards.

Towards the end of that semester, I gathered a couple of friends together to play music with. My Lindenwood friend, Roger Mayden, who had known Kim, was an avid songwriter, singer and could half-way play keyboards. His brother, Kerry Mayden, played drums. And my old friend Jim Koksal had acquired a bass guitar and a great Fender Bassman Amp. I set us up on the stage in the Fine Arts building, and we started playing around. Roger had a lot of songs, so we did several of his.

I introduced them to **"I Know A Song,"** so we did that one too. And then Jim said "Hey, why don't we try **"Sweet Attraction?"** Wow. I couldn't believe he even remembered that song. That had been on a demo tape I did in 1977, before Kim. But he remembered it, and I did too, so we did that as well. I might never have thought of that song again for the rest of my life had he not brought it up that night. I had been writing and recording songs over the years and only a few people would hear them. Haans and Jim heard them, and maybe Kevin Smith, Mark Snow and Pat Pfaff. Whoever was around at the time. I don't know how many of those Kim heard. Maybe all, maybe none. I'd write and record a song the same day. **"Sweet Attraction"** was about how young girls do things to attract attention to themselves with guys. Basically girls being girls. The deep, underlying theme was that of feminism actually. You don't have to put on makeup and wear certain clothes to be attractive. Attraction is more than physical. And it demeans woman to a certain point, when they overdo it. Think of John Lennon's song **"Woman Is The Nigger Of The World."** The line *"**We make them paint their face and dance…**"* Things haven't changed that much since the Cahokia

Mounds days, really, perhaps. So we did **"Sweet Attraction."**

We were rehearsing in the little theater of the Fine Arts Building. There was a stage and theater seating that went up. It was the same stage where I had first seen Kim do ballet. But there were no conscious thoughts of Kim. We were just messing around really. But we were having a great time.

Mark got hold of me and I told him what I was doing so he came over to hear us play one night. He thought the musicianship was definitely lacking, but it was still interesting. Jim, in particular, was pretty bad. So Mark asked Jim if he could play his bass. It happened just like that. Mark started playing bass. And on one of Roger's songs, Mark played guitar, and I played bass. Jim took it pretty well, but I kind of felt sorry for the guy. But we weren't really that serious about it. And my old roommate David showed up and he played viola. Then I got a phone call one night at the radio station from a lady who was organizing a large outdoor community festival in St. Charles. She asked if I knew of any bands that might like to play at the event. "Sure," I said. "I have a band. They're called **'Modern Life.'"** That was the title of a

Roger Mayden song we were doing. So I committed us to play this show without even consulting the other members of the band.

Modern Life playing the first Bastile Day Festival in St. Charles, 1982.
From left to right, Mark Snow, David, Roger Mayden and me.
You can see Kerry Mayden's leg and arms, on drums.

We weren't even a real band. And we didn't have the equipment we needed to play a big outdoor show. But you know what? We pulled it off anyway. Just like I'd done years earlier at that junior high school talent show. I phoned my old friend Kevin Smith and arranged to borrow his big guitar amp. And suddenly, our rehearsals became more serious. I wasn't worried about it at all. But Mark was sweating bullets. He told me many years later that the only reason he did it was because of me. Poor Mark. He still felt guilty for dropping out of **The Individuals** when we were fourteen. I put him through hell over that show I guess. But it went just fine in the end.

The lady who was organizing the event made arrangements to meet us downtown St. Charles one day to take publicity photos. She took some great black and whites of us outside on Main Street. Mark didn't show up. But me, Roger, Kerry, and David did. We were just having fun with it. As the date closed in for the show, Mark was becoming more and more nervous and expressed his discomfort to me with our lack of talent as a band, but I just kept assuring him that everything would be all right. We only practiced a couple of times a week, and I understood his concern. But it would be okay, I told him.

Mayor Boschert spoke just before we played. The Boscherts were a big family with a long history in St. Charles. One of his nieces was a Lindenwood student, and had been a friend of mine. I had been to her house a few years earlier many times. That was where Cathy lived. And they had a pot plant that was at least two feet tall. Funny that I had gotten busted for a two-inch pot plant. But now there I was onstage standing behind the Mayor, and it was difficult for me to keep a straight face. I wanted to make funny faces or something. It was authority on stage with rock and roll. It seemed a bit ironic to me. We did about eight songs. Two of mine, **"I Know A Song"** and **"Sweet Attraction,"** a cover of Johnny Cash's **"I Walk The Line"** which we did in the style of **The Clash**, like they'd done with **"I Fought The Law"** and the rest were Roger's songs. **"I Walk The Line"** was my idea to do. You can't go wrong with a Johnny Cash song. It was a great fun. Some of our college friends came to see us. My Mother was there and recorded it on my little portable cassette recorder. It wasn't awful, put it that way. Mark and I listened to that tape many times over the years and got a good laugh out of it. I am glad we did it. And I think he was too. But he told me many years later that the only reason he did was because he still felt guilty for backing out on me at the talent show in junior high school.

Mark and me onstage with Modern Life. Notice he is incognito. I played bass on this song and loved every minute of it.

I bought a yellow Fiat X 1/9 that next year. An incredible little Italian made sports car. Man, that car was fun. I loved that thing. I got it up to 120 mph a few times on the highway. And it was tiny. Sat about three inches off the ground. Cool as hell. I am lucky I didn't kill myself in that thing.

For some reason, I walked to a convenience store down the street from the college late one night, and while I was walking back, this girl drove up and asked me if I wanted a ride. I had actually seen her in the store. And apparently she saw me. She was really pretty, so I said "Yeah, sure." Her name was Janette, and that would lead to a friendship that lasts to this day. She was immediately attracted to the way I looked. I had on all black, including a black Frank Sinatra type hat. I often dressed in all black. Not like Goth though. One of my radio station buddies started calling me Johnny Cash as a joke. Sometimes I wore all white. I still had the long blonde hair, but not quite as long as it had been. So I did stick out in a crowd. More so at Lindenwood than Webster.

My whole Lindenwood College days never led to a serious relationship. I think that was partly because I was a little worried about getting into one after what had happened with Kim. And I just never met anyone that shook me.

There was a very pretty Japanese student there that I took out one time. We went down to Vintage Vinyl, the hip record store in University City. On our way, I was trying to make conversation, but her English wasn't that good. I was trying to talk to her about music, and I asked her if she liked **The Police** or **The Cars**. She quickly turned around and looked out of the back windshield and said "Police Cars?!!" No kidding. Poor girl. And there were a few others. But one in particular is well worth noting.

I met Annie in my Art Appreciation class. She was blonde and beautiful, and we became fast friends. I had a major crush on her. She was a few years older and had her own house near Lindenwood. Everybody seemed to love Annie, and a lot of the young college guys swooned over her. But she spent as much or more time with me than anyone. She had a great, positive outlook on life and was just fun to be around. And she appreciated me as an artist. I wrote her a few poems, and she loved them. She even hung one up in her bathroom, so she could start her mornings with a reminder that someone really cared for her, she told me later. And when Halloween of 1981 rolled around, it was me that she asked to go with her to a big outside party in the country. She said she would take care of both of our costumes. We would be going as Mount St. Helen, she explained. I'll never forget the site of her in her backyard as I drove up to her house earlier that day. There she was with wood, chicken wire, newspapers, paste and paint, making an eight foot tall replica of the infamous volcano. We would hide inside it, she said, and that would be our costume. What a great lady, she was. But it never became anything more than a friendship. And slowly we just stopped seeing each other.

I got a job after college at a retail store that sold computers. Only IBM and Apple. They were a local upscale company and had three locations. I didn't know anything about computers, but quickly learned. The company was having a big dinner/event in downtown St. Louis, and I wanted to bring a date. So I asked my friend Janette if she would go with me. It was on a Saturday night, and she had plans, as always, to go see some local hair band. I had spent a lot of time around Janette's house, and knew her younger sister named Kimmie, and her best friend, a girl named Julie. She was a lot younger than me. She had just graduated high school. But I asked Julie anyway. I really didn't want to go by myself. And she said yes. But she was concerned about how Janette would feel about that, even though Janette and I weren't girlfriend/boyfriend. So I told her we would keep it a secret. I went into work the next day and told my boss I would be coming to the party with a date. "Ok," he said, handing me the sign-up sheet. I had to write my date's name down. It suddenly dawned on me, I didn't know Julie's last name! So I just wrote "Julie O."

The party was great, and I was very happy that Julie agreed to go with me. Julie was probably only 18, and very good-looking. She was short and blonde, with big beautiful eyes. The most stunning eyes I had ever seen. Like a cupie doll. Her hair was short. She was big busted. Put it this way, I saw her on her high school graduation night, and someone had written "Jugs" on the windshield of her car. It was sort of a kidding nickname. I didn't plan to continue a relationship with Julie. Until after that first date. Something magic happened that night.

I hadn't really gone out with that many girls since Kim. But I really enjoyed being with Julie, and so we started seeing each other, day by day. Before I knew it, I was falling in love.

Julie wasn't like Kim. But they shared a few physical similarities. Julie wasn't a straight A student nor the most ambitious person in the world. She was more like me. But she was fun, and before long, we grew to love each other. We became inseparable. It wasn't long until she didn't care if Janette knew we were going out. And then we went together everywhere, even to Janette's house. For the first time since Kim, I was in a serious relationship. It had taken three years.

Julie was the first and only child of the marriage between her Mother and Father, and at some point early in her life, that marriage ended. Her Mother remarried, and had a daughter a few years later. So she had a half-sister about 3 or 4 years younger than her by her stepfather. So it was in that household that I would go see Julie, and her stepfather worked nights and was a bit of an asshole, I thought. If anyone was too loud, he would come storming out of his room yelling. And one time, Julie and I went into her bedroom, and her step-father insisted that we keep the bedroom door open. Like we were going to be doing something. It was weird.

I guess I can't blame him. He didn't know me, and I was way older than her. I think his name was Frank. He didn't care much for me for some reason. But I didn't really care. He was an asshole. I had experience with step-fathers.

Julie came over to my house every weekend. We did everything together. We got season passes to Six Flags. We had so much fun. I was happy again. Finally.

I have so many fond memories of those days. I took her on a float trip one time in the Summer, and she perched on the front of the canoe like a little queen, while I paddled in the back. It made me feel good again. On our way home that night, she fell asleep in the car. And that is a magical memory. It dawned on me at that very moment that this young girl loved me and completely trusted me to take care of her. It was the first time since Kim that

I had felt that. And it was a good feeling to get back.

We went to a hot tub rental place one time. You could rent an hour in a private hot tub surrounded by tall wooden walls. We made love in that hot tub and it was incredible. You don't forget something like that.

That Christmas, I had no idea what to get her. I walked around a mall at the last minute, and ended up buying her a white, sleeveless fur coat. It looked cool as hell, I thought. And when we had Christmas at my parent's house, I gave it to her. She was thrilled. And she cried. I have a small photo of that. Julie with that white fur coat on Christmas Day, crying.

She would spend the night with me at my parent's house on weekends. They had bought a nice big house in St. Peter's, Missouri. It was not the same house that we had when I was with Kim. It was a two-story house, with a vaulted ceiling, two bedrooms, a bathroom and living room upstairs. That whole upstairs was pretty much ours. Julie loved me and I loved her. Just like that. I believed in magic again. And it was amazing.

I got a call from Julie one day at work that I will never forget. She said, "I just called. . . to say. . . I love you." She was quoting the Stevie Wonder song. "Oh, thank you!" I said, "I love you too." It took me years to really appreciate the significance of that phone call. I thought it was very lovely at the time, but once again, that is something that has stuck with me after all these years. No one had ever done that for me before or since. The little things. Like a phone call for no reason other than to say "I love you."

Julie wanted us to get our own place together. She dropped the hint that we should check out a certain apartment complex. I didn't do anything with that information. I wasn't quite ready to make rental payments, and she was still going to cosmetology school. I was dodging it. I was not quite ready to make that commitment.

We went to Janette and Kimmie's house one night, and by then, Kimmie was married to a nice guy also named Steve. Julie had been friends with Kimmie for a long time by then, and we often went there and hung out with them a small group of friends. It was a completely separate life than I'd had four years earlier with Kim Jordan. With me and Kim, it was a bit more private. We spent a lot of time alone together. Julie was a bit more social and definitely more of a party girl. All of a sudden, I found Julie and Steve in the living room standing very close. It was the strangest thing. They were flirting. I don't remember how much we'd had to drink by then, but I saw this, and walked up to them and they just continued to stand, very close together. I said something like "What are you doing?" And she didn't answer me. "Ok," I said, "let's go." I made it clear I was upset. I was actually really pissed off. This was her best friend's husband. But Kimmie didn't see what was going on and acted like I was crazy. I drove Julie home, and the when she tried to explain, all I would say is "I'm just taking you home and dropping you off!" I repeated it several times on the ten-minute drive. She actually laughed about it later and would quote me, "I'm just taking you home and dropping you off!" I am glad she thought it was funny because I did not. Maybe I was over-reacting. But I don't think so. This was my girlfriend. He was married to her best friend. They had no business doing that, I thought.

She was young. Twenty years old by then. I must have been around 25 or 26. Seems like a big age difference. I don't know what the hell I was thinking.

Julie had to have some major root canal done and I had arranged to take her to the dentist and be there for her. When she got in the chair, the dentist read her the crazy stuff they have to read about possible bad things that could happen, etc. and she started freaking out and crying. I held her hand and assured her everything would be fine. I was there for her. Like I had been for Kim. I had her back. But it didn't matter; the dentist didn't even get started. I drove her back to her house and as soon as we got in the car, she stopped crying and acted like nothing happened. I did the same. We never talked about it again. That is one of those incidents, like when Kim was sick and in the hospital, when I was there for her. It may sound trivial, but it's not. You have to have each other's back, I thought. That is what love is really all about. It's not just the emotions, it's the actions. In good times and bad. I believed in all of that.

Julie was into Prince at the time. Had his poster on the wall and played the album **"Purple Rain."** She took me into her room, and played me that LP for the first time. It was good. Not my cup of tea, but it was okay. I think her favorite song was **"Little Red Corvette."** Truth is, I was actually a bit jealous of her fascination with Prince. I went out and got a poster of Christy Brinkley and hung it up in my room just to make a point. She didn't think it was funny. Her step dad came banging on the door and made us keep it open. I guess he was afraid we were going to have sex in her room. It was like I was 16 or something. I didn't particularly like that guy. But usually, we got along fine. Then again, we rarely went into her room and closed the door. I remembered when I had gone to Kim's house in Wickford. I stayed in her room and she slept upstairs on the couch.

I had gotten a tape of a bootleg of **The Beatle's "Strawberry Field's Forever"** which was the first take they did. It was drastically different from what came out, and I was excited as hell about it. It was much faster and just incredible to hear. So I took it over to Julie's house with my little portable cassette player. We sat at her kitchen table and I played it for her and her little sister, explaining it's importance, and so on. Her step dad worked nights. So I guess we woke him up, because he came barreling into the kitchen and said something like "The next person who wakes me up is going in the pool!" Meaning he would throw us into the pool they had in their backyard. I wasn't playing it that loud. The guy could be a jerk.

Rap music was just coming out big, and Julie loved it. I did not. That caused a bit of riff sometimes in the car because she would change my rock and roll radio station to a rap station. I could put up with it for a while, but then would have to change it back. One day she told me she wanted to go to a show that was coming to The Fox Theater in St. Louis. It was **New Edition**. I didn't know or care who they were. All I knew is it was some young black singing group. Also on the bill were **The Fat Boys** and **UTFO**, two rap groups. I reluctantly bought us tickets, and she was thrilled to death! I think we were the only white people in the audience. But I have to admit; I kind of enjoyed the show. It was certainly interesting. And I am thankful to her to this day for that experience. I would have never gone had it not been for Julie.

Someone stopped Julie and I as we were going into Six-Flags one day and took our picture. Then as we were leaving the park that day, they sold us that picture in a little plastic looking glass thing. I bought it, of course. I had it for years. I don't know what ever happened to that. Just as we were walking out, the sky opened up and it poured rain. We ran to the car and jumped inside. I gave Julie something to dry off with and we drove home, happy, tired, in love and wet! Julie was beautiful inside and out. And I loved her.

Julie came over one Saturday morning as usual. But this time instead of talking about what we would do that day, she started talking about something else. I don't remember what she said exactly, but she was breaking up with me. She was about to turn 21 and I think she wanted to go out and have fun. I don't recall either what I said in response. I didn't get mad. We didn't argue, I know that. But I wasn't expecting it. She walked out of the house and I went upstairs to the bathroom. Then I hit the shower door with my fist and thought, "Damn! Not again!" That was pretty much it for me. I would never love another woman quite the same way again. Names and dates all change. And when you see me staring off, and wondering what I'm thinking of, it's doubtful that I'm in the past, vague memories through the broken glass.

Julie and me at my parent's house, 1984. This would be the last serious relationship I would have for many years.

Chapter Eight

So I took a deep breath, and dialed her number. And suddenly, I was talking to Kim Jordan again.

Julie was gone and I didn't know what to do with myself. Like Kim before her, she was pretty much my whole life. We had spent nearly every day together for a year and a half. It dawned on me later that our relationship lasted about as long as mine had with Kim. A year and a half. It seemed like a damn curse or something. And I went through the same emotions as I had with Kim. *What the hell am I going to do now?* So out of sheer boredom, one night I called my old friend Roger Mayden. That one phone call would change my life.

Roger told me that he was singing and writing songs in a band called **The Eighth Day** and asked if I wanted to come hear them rehearse. "Hell yes!" I said. I had dropped out of the local music scene several years earlier and was desperate to do something! Anything! So I went to hear them practice one night.

The Eighth Day rehearsed in the basement of the

keyboard player, Eric Svoboda. Eric had just graduated high school so he was much younger than Roger and I. The only other band member was a kid about Eric's age named Brian Schwartzentruber. He was the drummer. That was it. They played techno pop, which I wasn't real crazy about, but they were quite good, I thought. All of the music was produced by Eric on a synthesizer and Roger's old "string machine" keyboard that we had used in **Modern Life**. I was immediately impressed by Eric. There were no guitars, which rubbed me the wrong way in principal, but the music was full of melody and great hooks. The drummer was quite good too, and Roger had come a long way vocally. "I may be on to something here," I thought. So it wasn't long before I offered to manage them. I would take 15% of whatever they earned. I knew that would probably equate to 15% of nothing. But if I could get them in front of the right people, and they got a recording contract and could tour, that 15% could potentially be pretty big. Then I would write a book about it. It was a million to one shot, but what the hell. I had heard plenty of other groups with less talent. So while certainly not likely, it was possible. And I wasn't doing anything else anyway. I saw an opportunity, and grabbed it by the goddamn throat and was determined to hang on for dear life. No contract was ever signed, but we made a verbal agreement. I was now the manager of **The Eighth Day**.

The original business card I had printed up included mine and Eric's phone number. That was all you needed back then. We were in business!

The first thing I did was get them some local gigs. That wasn't an easy task in St. Louis in 1985. There were very few venues that would book bands that did original material. Let alone techno pop, even though that genre was climbing in the charts at that time. Missouri was still a bit backward and late to jump on the bandwagon. But I did manage to get them a few shows. One was at a place called Turner's. They would share the bill with a couple other groups and there were probably only a hundred kids there. But it gave them some experience playing live shows. By then a high school friend of Eric's, a girl named Tracy, was singing back- up vocals. It was a nice addition, but she wasn't really an official member of the band. But she was a big fan and fun to be around. I liked Tracy.

I moved them from Eric's basement to Lindenwood College to rehearse. We used the same Fine Art's building theater that I used for **Modern Life**. The same stage I'd seen Kim do ballet for the first time. And again there were no thoughts of Kim Jordan. I didn't think about her. It had been five years since our breakup but it seemed like a lifetime ago. Sometimes I would operate the stage lights and they would run through their songs one right after another, as if they were doing a live show. I stressed the importance of very short pauses between songs. It helped them get serious about it.

We played a popular club downtown St. Louis called "Mississippi Nights." Granted, it was an original songs package show and there were 10 other acts on the bill, but it was still an accomplishment. And it made me realize just how good they had become in a short period of time. They were more interesting than the other local groups. The songs were good. You could whistle the melodies. Eric and Roger were becoming good songwriting partners. It was quite impressive. They were ready, I thought, to go pro.

One night at a rehearsal at Lindenwood, I told the guys to take a break. "We have to move," I said. "We have to get out of St. Louis." I felt we had done all we could do there. "We have to go to either the East Coast or the West Coast, but we can't stay here" I said. "So what'll it be guys?" They looked at me dumbfounded, but they knew I was as serious as a heart attack. It was time to shit or get off the pot. Tracy, our background singer and good friend and supporter, was going off to Boston

University. She agreed to let us stay with her in her dorm room until we found a band house. So it was decided. We would go to the East coast.

The Fine Arts Building, Lindenwood College, where I first saw Kim dance. I would go on to take dance classes in the very same building and rehearse The Eighth Day.

We packed all of the band equipment into my Ford pickup truck. It had a camper shell on it so it was locked and safe. The drummer, Brian, had bought a set of electronic drums that you play like regular drums but you could change the sound of them through a little console. We ran everything through one power source, one mixer and one P.A. system. That meant we could set up and do a show in less than an hour. All of that equipment fit in the back of my truck. Brian and I drove straight through from St. Louis to Boston without stopping. It took 24 hours. I drove most of the way. By the time we got to B.U., we were exhausted. But we managed to find Tracy and signed in for a three-day pass to stay with her and her roommate in their dorm. Eric and Roger would follow a couple of days later.

Boston University was a great place to live. We stayed in one of the three high rise dorms that surround the football stadium. The place was huge. The plan was we would say at B.U. until we could find a house to rent. So we just kept signing up for three day "passes" while Roger and I searched for a house. Unbelievably, Tracy's roommate didn't mind us staying at all. Like Tracy, she was a freshman, and actually loved the idea of having a band staying in her room. We were sleeping on the floor between their twin beds. It sounds nuts now, and it kind of was. Four guys crashing with two girls in a little dorm room. We were probably there for two or three weeks. But unlike me sneaking in and our of Kim's dorm at Webster, this was on the up and up. We were legal guests, but we were pushing our welcome as far as the University was concerned.

Since we were on the East Coast, Kim popped into my mind. She's from Rhode Island. Maybe she still lives here. And for the first time since our breakup, I decided I would try to get in touch with her. She could have been anywhere. I didn't know. But I wanted to contact her. So I called her Mother. She remembered me, of course, and put me in touch with Kim. So I called Kim. And she seemed to be happy to hear from me! I told her what I was doing, why I was in Boston, and we arranged to meet for lunch. It was unbelievable to me. She was living in the Boston area too, as I recall. She gave me the name and location of a little restaurant, and we set a date and time to meet. I took the mass transit subway, or "T" as they call it, and found my way to the café. I was anxious to meet with her but had mixed emotions. Six years had passed and I found myself sitting across a table from Kim Jordan. Words can't capture it. It was almost surreal. I did a good job of hiding my emotions, and we just had a nice, long chat. Like old friends. And I don't remember much of the conversation. I have this very vivid memory of her listening to me talk in deep concentration. She had her right hand on the side of her face, index finger on her temple, listening intently. I was telling her what I was doing, and I asked her something like "Do you remember Roger?" or something like that, and she said, "I don't remember anything!" and laughed. She was exaggerating, of course, but it is ironically the only thing that I remember that she said. It hurt my feelings. I know she was kidding, and it was an expression, but it hurt me. "I remember everything," I said. She picked up the check and I let her. We left the restaurant and said our goodbyes on the sidewalk out in front of the café. I don't remember if we hugged or not. We probably did. It took everything I had to hold back the tears. And as we went our separate ways, I stopped and turned around. I watched Kim walk down that sidewalk and away from me and all of the loss and sorrow came rushing back. I wanted to yell out "Kim! I love you!" But I did not. Instead I quietly watched her walk away from me until she made a right turn onto another street and out of sight. I got back on the subway, tears slowly trickling down my cheeks in a car full of strangers.

From left to right, Eric Svoboda and Roger Mayden in concert.

In the nick of time, **The Eighth Day** found a house on Martha's Vineyard. It was a winter rental, so it was cheap. $450 a month. Roger and I took the ferry to the Island to check it out, and we were immediately impressed. The Boston music scene was twenty times bigger than St. Louis, and I decided we needed more work, and the Vineyard would be a good place to do that. I had made a few contacts in Boston, but realized that maybe we weren't quite as ready as I had thought we were. So I moved the group to Martha's Vineyard and they went to work on writing new songs.

And write they did. They came up with their best songs yet, I thought, on The Vineyard. To keep them motivated, I arranged for a live show that winter. I booked the historic Catherine Cornell Theater for one night for $35. and began the promotional process for the concert. We had made friends on the island by then, including some high school girls who by word of mouth would promote the show for us. But only about 40 kids showed up. It was a small community. The show went well, despite the lack of audience. They wrote six or so songs in a short period of time, and each one was better than the one before. Tracy would come down for the weekend, and ended up dropping out of B.U. and moving down to be with the band full-time. I was against that move because her and Roger had become a couple. We had many discussions about it. I didn't want her to drop out of college, and I didn't want **The Eighth Day** to become a group fronted by a male and female couple that were the singers. Brian agreed with me, but Eric was a bit more neutral as I recall, pointing out that it might actually be good for the group. Some of the girls on the island thought Tracy was cool as hell, so maybe Roger and Eric were right. I just didn't think so. And the idea of her and Roger being a couple concerned me. What if they broke up? It would be the end of the group. So I fought it tooth and nail. But in the end, I was not in control. Kim had told me one time that I needed to learn how to say no. I certainly learned that. I was saying no with a lot of adjectives thrown in. I was a fighter. Kim would be proud, I thought. But not only had I learned how to say no, I learned how to lean on it and be an asshole when I had to be. **You've got to give the other fellow hell!** just as Kim had quoted Paul McCartney six or so years earlier. It's funny, but Kim taught me a lot. It just took years for me to get it.

The Winter came and passed and it was time for **The Eighth Day** to move off of the Island. I was pretty much done with them by then, having convinced myself that the direction of the band with Tracy was wrong and ill fated. But I helped Eric and Brian find an apartment in Little Italy, and Roger and Tracy took an apartment together in a Boston suburb. I arranged for one last show in the Boston area, and sent out over 100 letters to various other bands, promoters and entertainment groups as invitations. I rented out a club and dressed the band up as priests. People had always mistakenly thought that the name of the band, **The Eighth Day**, had something to do with religion. The name had actually come from watching a Clearasil commercial on TV. Day One, and they show the kids face, a lot of acne, Day Two, a little less, and so forth to Day Seven, and one of them said "Day Eight!" And someone else said **"The Eighth Day!"** And that was it. No one showed up at that last show in Boston. Well, I think there were three people there besides the band and staff. It was a great show, though. They did a good show. I had failed in getting them in front of someone who mattered. It was harder to control the band than I'd imagined. I would keep in touch with them and perhaps join them at a later time. If they were to get a break, they would need someone they could absolutely trust. That would be me. I would be their umbrella. After that show, I went back to Martha's Vineyard. I would stay there for six more years.

Brian the drummer. He was the first drummer I'd ever met who played an all synthesized kit.

The Eighth Day had taken me from St. Louis to Martha's Vineyard. I really liked living there. It was laid back and very beautiful. It reminded me of Block Island, where Kim had taken me that fated trip to Rhode Island seven years previously. It crossed my mind to call Kim again in 1987 when **The Eighth Day** had ran its course, but I didn't. I had to go on with my life, and now I had no girlfriend and no band. And I was a thousand miles from home. I loved The Vineyard and made it my sanctuary. I did house painting, which is what we had done when we first got there as a group to pay the bills. I met new friends on my own and had a lot of adventures. My sister, Tina, ended up moving out there and we got a house together. And I bought a set of drums. The first set I had owned since Kim Jordan, and started playing music myself again. I was suddenly in a band again, and I named us **The Dirty Dogs**. It was straightforward rock and roll, down and dirty, like the good old days. And for no good reason other than to play music. We had a singer, guitarist, bassist and drummer. I was the drummer. Again. I wasn't that worried about getting gigs or anything, but we did play out a bit and just had fun. I had long hair again. Longer than I'd ever had it before. It was down past my shoulders. And I was playing the shit out of the drums, with a passion. "To the max," as I would say to Kim in the old days. By then, I was a ten-year war veteran as far as playing drums goes. And we were playing mostly original songs, although none of mine. The singer was incredibly passionate about rock and roll. His name was Ricky Padilla. A second generation Cuban transplant from Miami, Florida. He was into Jim Morrison, but I turned him on to Iggy Pop, and there was no stopping him after that. He was a lot younger than I was, so I enjoyed seeing him learn new things that I had already experienced. Kind of like a younger brother in a way. It was great seeing that energy again. And it made him and the guitarist encourage me not just to play the drums again, but to beat the hell out of them. And I did.

The Dirty Dogs played a house party one night, and Roger came down from Boston that weekend and sang a few songs, including Lou Reed's **"Sweet Jane."** It was great fun. It was a birthday party for Maggie, a college girl (which means she wasn't from the island).

She was a friend that worked at the Black Dog

Bakery. The performance was subsequently bootlegged on a small scale. We played for what seemed like three hours straight. I wish I had that tape now. It was from my tape recorder that the bootleg was taken. **"The Dirty Dogs Live From Maggie's."** But **The Dogs** were short lived, like most good rock bands. Ricky went on to form anther group called **The Endorphins**. They eventually broke up too.

I went on to manage an old fashioned bookstore/newsstand that had just opened up on The Vineyard called The Hub 2. The original Hub bookstore had been opened on Nantucket for many years. The company that owned it wanted to open one on the Vineyard too. So I was interviewed for the job and got the position. Janette came to visit me that summer. She stayed for two weeks. It was great having her there, and I showed her all around the Island. To this day, she says it was the best lobster she has ever had. Janette was such a great friend. But we were just friends. It was nice to have her there though, but when she left, I felt lonely.

Looking up at the castle. I don't remember looking up at it then, but I am sure I did. I just remember walking in and out. Vague memories through the broken glass.

Seemingly out of the blue, I called Kim's Mom, Jan Jordan one night. It had been four years since I had talked to her, but it seemed like it had been the week before. Of course, she said, she remembered me, and gave me Kim's phone number. I don't think we talked for more than a couple of minutes. But she was very nice to me. I will always have a soft spot in my heart for that woman.

So I called Kim. It took me awhile to do that. Maybe an hour, maybe a few days. I am not sure. But it was an important phone call in my mind. So I took a deep breath, and dialed her number. And suddenly, I was talking to Kim Jordan again. Like the lunch meeting we had, I only remember a couple of things about our conversation. She seemed to be happy to hear from me, but actually all I remember is her telling me she was going to be getting married. Anything else she said is lost on me to this day. *We* were supposed to be getting married! Had we gotten married when we planned, we would have been married for seven years. "What the hell happened?" I thought. She said her and her fiancé might come down soon to Martha's Vineyard, and if so, they would look me up. Oh God, I hoped not! I would have loved to see her again, but I couldn't have handled seeing her with another guy. That would have killed me. So I am glad it never happened. That would be the last phone conversation I would have with Kim Jordan. She never got back with me. It was 1989. The Eighties were about to end.

Chapter Nine

Slowly life goes on, yet quickly time passes. Names and dates all change. I found myself with a son I never asked for, yet couldn't imagine myself living without.

I got on with my life post-Kim as usual. It was really nice talking to her though. I just couldn't think about it much, and I didn't. I figured that was it. It had been ten years since we split. A lifetime, really. How much longer would she sneak into my consciousness? Would this never end? I went about my life and tried not to think about such craziness.

My parents came to visit me on the island that year. They drove out, and took the opportunity to bring me a few things that I had left at their home for years and years. A box of reel-to-reel tapes, some albums, and that big box of Kim's letters she had sent to me the Summer of 1979. Holy shit! I carefully opened the lid and looked inside, and there they were. They weren't lined up in pretty rows, mind you, but just as I'd left them, tossed in as I'd received them. I don't know how many, but I swear it must have been nearly a hundred letters. There were probably photos in there too, I don't remember. I hadn't read any of them in I don't know how many years. It was like a shrine. I didn't want to read them but couldn't bring myself to throw them away either. I just put the lid back on and stuck the box under my bed. Like I had always done.

The bookstore that I worked for changed ownership so I took a job as an appetizer chef in a French restaurant called Le Greiner. My roommate, Steve Koult, was the head chef there, along with the owner, Jean Dupont. It was a great learning experience. These days, culinary students would pay to work there. I got paid and learned a lot in my two years there. And it was certainly different. I had done a lot on the island. Had a lot of great experiences. I had painted houses, ran a bookstore, and worked in a restaurant. I'd met a lot of famous people on a casual basis. Carly Simon, Walter Cronkite, Judy Belushi, Mike Wallace, to name a few. Walter Cronkite use to come into the bookstore and talk to my cockatiel, my pet bird that I had in a cage on the counter. "Hello Nester," he would say, as I quietly freaked out. "Walter Cronkite is standing here scratching my cockatiel's head!" I would be thinking. I'd seen John F. Kennedy Jr. a few times, and Jackie Onassis once, up close and personal. It was just part of living on The Vineyard. I had met a lot of girls, gone out on a lot of dates, but it ran its course. Had I met and fell in love with a girl there, I would probably be on Martha's Vineyard today. It just didn't happen for me. So I decided I would move back to St. Louis and start over.

I didn't have a lot of material possessions. Mostly clothes. Since I was driving back, that was a good thing. Space was limited in the car, so I got rid of a lot of things. Including that box of letters from Kim. I will never forget tossing that box into the outside trashcan. It was a pretty big box. It held a lot of memories. It was very symbolic to me. I did it quickly and tried not to look at the box as I closed the trashcan lid. I don't remember if my cheeks were wet with tears or not. I think I was able to suppress that this time. I finally got rid of the letters. It was a huge deal to me. I'd had them for more than fourteen years.

I took my time and reflected on my life on that drive back from Martha's Vineyard to St. Louis that Spring. Seven years earlier, Brian and I made that drive straight through in 24 hours. I took three days this time. I wasn't in any hurry really. I was alone and didn't have any plans. When I did get back, I was greeted with the largest flood in over 100 years. The Great Flood of 1993 was waiting for me. It was crazy, but didn't directly affect me. I did help do some sandbagging one day though, and that nearly killed me. I had been through two hurricanes on Martha's Vineyard, but I had never seen anything quite like that flood. It was devastating.

I took a job with a company in St. Charles that provided services to people with developmental disabilities. It just seemed like the right thing to do at the time. I quickly moved up to a management position, but that ended after a year or so when I went the other way and took a job at a casino in customer service. I did a fair amount of socializing, still looking for that special someone, and ended up going out with a super outgoing black girl and aspiring singer named Michelle Ashley. And she could sing! I don't remember when we met. Probably 1995. And I have to be honest and say it wasn't love at first sight for either of us. We took things slowly. Especially me. And when things seemed to be getting a bit too serious, I broke it off with her. I had never done that before. It just didn't seem quite right, though. I didn't know what I was doing. I was different. I was pushing forty and still didn't know what I wanted. I was content with being single. In fact, I rather enjoyed it. I was not unhappy. And maybe I just didn't trust being in a serious relationship. I had learned a hard lesson. And that comes with experience and time. I wasn't twenty-one anymore. Nothing would impact me the same way as it did then. So I drifted. But I did go back to Michelle. I don't know where the years went but 1993 turned into 1998 almost overnight. I had moved into Michelle's apartment with her and she started talking about getting married. And after a year and a half of planning, on March 11th, 2000, we did just that. It was a pretty big wedding, and Eric Svoboda and Roger Mayden were in our wedding party. Also Haans Peterson and Mark Snow. Haans was my best man. Michelle sang **"In My Life"** at our wedding reception. It was great. And our wedding dance at the reception was done to the Elvis Costello/Burt Bacharach song **"She."** It was still the Beatles and Elvis Costello for me.

That wasn't going to change. But my life sure did.

We were at my parent's house for dinner one night when my Mother explained that an old friend of her's had a grandaughter who pregnant and wanting to give the baby up for adoption. "Would you be interested?" she asked us. "Hell yes!" was our response. Michelle was trying to get pregnant. She really wanted to have a baby. I went along with it with mixed feelings, but it wasn't happening, physically. And suddenly, here, dropped in our laps, was an opportunity for a child. The birth mother was only seventeen and this was her second pregnancy. She already had a baby girl and knew she couldn't take care of another. So we agreed to have her over for a weekend and let her decide if she wanted us to be the parents of her unborn child. It was strange. But we were excited of the prospect. The young girl, named Candice, came and at the end of the weekend said yes, that is what she wanted to do. She would sign over papers for Michelle and I to be the child's parents. But then weeks and months went by and we didn't hear from her, so we just thought she had changed her mind. It was too good and easy to be true, I thought. Then one night the phone rang, and it was Candice.

"I can't take it anymore! I want you to come get this baby!" she cried. I handed the phone to Michelle. After calming Candice down, Michelle explained that we had to call our lawyer first and that we would get back to her right away. So the next morning, Michelle called a lawyer her family had used. "Do you want the baby?" he asked. "Yes." Michelle said. "Then go get the baby and we will take care of it." The birthmother had called us on a Wednesday. We picked him up that Friday. He was 32 days old. We have had him ever since.

Since we had no time to prepare to have a baby, the first stop we made with him was at the grocery store to get baby stuff. Formula and so forth. Most couples have at least months to prepare. We had two days! I pulled a drawer out of our chest of drawers and carefully lined it with a sheet and a large pillow. He slept in that until we could get a proper crib. Literally overnight, I was a Father. It was as if there were a God and that God said "Here!" It was the most amazing thing! We had been wanting a child, she was trying to get pregnant, but it wasn't happening. We had seen the opportunity to have one by adoption and then it disappeared, then like a flash, came back! Just that quickly. We had a son. We named him Justin Michael Ashley-Thomas. The first and middle name was Michelle's idea. The hyphenated last name was mine. This child was a gift, and he would have both our names. It was a very John Lennon thing to do.

"But I don't want to have any babies" she explained. I didn't even question that, but I might have said something like "You don't want any children?" "Well, we could adopt a five year old. Maybe a little black boy," she replied.

It didn't dawn on me until this writing how eerily ironic that statement Kim had made to me 23 years earlier had become. My son Justin was adopted, a boy and of mixed ethnicity. I didn't get Kim, but I got that son she talked about 23 years earlier.

I took to being a Father with surprising gusto. It was unexpected, and all or nothing. For me, it was everything all at once. I was 44 years old. Old enough to be a grandparent, technically. But a lot more experienced than younger parents, and certainly more appreciative than some. This was the biggest thing that had ever happened to me. I was responsible for a baby. I got up when he cried and made a bottle. I changed his diapers and fed him. I learned how to rock him, to burp him, everything. And one night I was holding him in my arms and very gently patting him on his little back. And suddenly, I felt this tiny hand. He was patting me back! It was incredible. I'll never forget that moment. Some people, some parents, look upon these things as a chore. I looked at it with great pride that this gift was bestowed upon me, and these are the things you have to do to take care of a baby. And despite the sleep deprivation, the work, it was worth it every day. Because this was my child. It was a different kind of love for me. And you can have friends who have children, you can have nephews or nieces, you can read about it in books, but until it happens to you first hand, you won't understand that kind of love. And it didn't matter to me that he was not my biological child. In fact, it made it that much more special. It was magic. Like with Kim, I wasn't looking for it, it just happened. It is magic. And I believed in magic.

Then one night the phone rang. It was the biological mother. All I remember her saying is "I want my baby back!" I handed the phone to Michelle, speechless. I didn't know how to handle it. So Michelle called the lawyer who handled the adoption. The birthmother also got a lawyer, and we found ourselves back in court battling for the right to keep my son. It turns out, the birthmother was not yet eighteen when she signed over her parental rights. And even though the judged signed off on the adoption, it was suddenly null and void. Justin was a year and a half old by then, and I couldn't imagine losing him then. Michelle and I went through hell, as did our families. We went to court several times, and it drug out for several months. The final time we went, we had to bring an extra bag of clothes and such for him in case family services decided to take him. It was the toughest thing I'd ever had to do. The reality of losing Justin was hitting me in the face. This couldn't be happening. But on that day, the birthmother caved. She signed adoption papers again, and this time she was eighteen years old. It was finally a done deal. I made a silent vow to myself on that day that no one would ever take my son away from me. I didn't think it was possible, but it made being his Father even that much more special. I would never take that gift for granted.

We bought a house but things weren't great on the home front between my wife and me. I busied myself taking care of the pool and the huge yard and looking after Justin, but my relationship with Michelle was deteriorating. We had been married for four years, together for probably seven. And out of the blue one day I thought, *I wonder how Kim is doing.* I picked up the phone and called Jan Jordan. It was 2004 or 2005. I explained to her who I was and was just wondering how Kim was doing. "She is the CEO of her own company in Germany," she told me. "Holy shit!" I thought, although I translated that to something like "Wow, that's great" when talking to her Mother. I told her that I was married, and how we ended up with Justin. She went on to explain that Kim was married too, but had no children. And for the third time over the course of nearly twenty years, she gave me Kim's phone number. I think I tried calling her a couple of times, but was worried what my wife would make of me calling Germany if she happened to see it on our phone bill. At any rate, I never talked to Kim. Talking to her Mother was somehow satisfying enough, and at least I knew Kim was all right and doing quite well apparently. It had been 15 years since I'd talked to Kim and her Mother. That's a hell of a lot of water under the bridge. Enough to fill the River Rhine.

Slowly life goes on, yet quickly time passes. Names and dates all change. I found myself with a son I never asked for, yet couldn't imagine myself living without.

He was just three years old when my wife and I separated. I had only lived in our house for eleven months when I moved out. Didn't even make it a year. But I was hopeful that I would be moving back in. And for the next six months, I tried, but it never happened. I ended up getting my own place, and realized I wasn't going to be going back. I had to keep moving forward like always. What kept me motivated to wake up in the morning was my son. He needed me. I worked four ten-hour days, so I was off on Friday, Saturday and Sunday. So I would pick him up on Thursday night and have him until Sunday evening or Monday morning. I have had him almost every weekend since then. I had him more than half the time. And that was great. I would just as soon have him all the time, but I realized he also needed his Mother. I was not going to be an every other weekend Father. I remembered how my own Father had been completely vacant from my life and I was not about to do that. I couldn't do that, and never understood how my Father could. I had effectively blocked that out of my consciousness, but it came to the forefront of my mind when I had my own son. My Father didn't need me, I concluded at an early age. But I needed my son. Perhaps more so than most Dads' think they need their son. That was the difference between my Father and myself. That was all I knew for sure. John Lennon's song **"Mother"** on **Plastic Ono Band** came to mind: **"Father you left me, but I never left you. I wanted you. You didn't want me. So I just gotta tell you. Goodbye. Goodbye."** I had suppressed those feelings. With my Father. With Kim. But sometimes those feelings and emotions come back. Kim left me too, just like my Father had. And I loved Kim more than I loved my own Father. The truth is, I never really knew him. I was about Justin's age when my parents separated. Two or three. So I didn't remember him, yet I knew he left me. And I didn't understand why. Just like I didn't understand why Kim left. But I was 21 when Kim left me, so that I remembered. So I drew parallels. I honed defense mechanisms. I would become a damn good Father-at least the best that I knew how to be. And I knew nothing other *than I will always love you, I will never leave you.* That would become my mantra.

Chapter Ten

That was all I wanted to do. Just write her one more letter. I wrote it off the top of my head in about ten minutes. It had been 33 years since we were together.

I didn't think I would ever get back in touch with Kim again after all these years, but I did. And like before, it came about in the strangest way. I was raising my son. Day by day. Nothing else mattered. Kim was the furthest thing from my mind. Yet always there somehow in the deep recesses of my subconscious.

When Justin was about three years old, we were watching a **Wiggle's** DVD, for the millionth time, and I decided I needed to see some **Beatles**. I had a lot of **Beatles** video, thanks to my lifelong friend, Mark Snow. So I played the first Ed Sullivan performance. That was what had made me a fan to begin with, like millions of others. To my astonishment, Justin was immediately mesmerized! Just as I had been as a child. I had an old pair of rabbit ear TV antennas sitting next to the TV, and he grabbed those and pulled on of the shafts up, to make a microphone stand, then picked up a long stick and used it as a guitar. He watched and mimicked their performance. And he wanted to watch it over and over again. That kid learned the words to all of those songs in short order and would pretend to be playing guitar. He did all the moves too. He was doing the Beatles. I was shocked and proud as hell as you can imagine. I invited my parent's over shortly thereafter to watch him do his Beatles impersonation. And I videotaped it. My parents were also amazed. My Mom took the videotape to a company in St. Charles that would transfer it onto a DVD disk. And the man that ran that company asked her "Who is that kid?" "My Grandson," she replied. "Well, I do a lot of theater and I have never seen a child that age so into a performance," he said. "That kid is very talented." My Mother beamed with pride. From then on, I slowly exposed him to other rock and roll music. He was hooked. At age five, he knew **The Beatles, The Rolling Stones, Bob Dylan**, etc. I played him the same music videos that I would normally watch. Justin was getting an education in rock and roll. As it should be. Over night, he had graduated from **The Wiggles** to **The Beatles**. It was amazing. But with me as Dad, it was bound to happen sooner or later. **KISS** came next, and he loved them.

I had seen **KISS** a couple of times when I was in high school. My first real rock concert though was **Aerosmith** in 1977. Tickets cost $8.50. And parking was free. I also saw **Queen** that year. And **The Beach Boys** with **Chicago**. And **The Rolling Stones**. Those were important times for me in 1977. I never dreamed that these bands would be popular and still touring some 30 years later. I would go on to see **The Rolling Stones** three more times in just a couple of months during their **"Voodoo Lounge"** tour in 1993. Tickets were still fairly reasonable in those days. But the coolest show I ever saw was Elvis Costello. And that was just before Kim, I think. Things happened very fast at the time and everything seemed very important. Dog days. Rapid fire. "Don't touch me now, I'm a real live wire." That is from **Talking Heads** song **"Psycho Killer."** Another band I saw early on. So all of this was going on just prior to meeting Kim. I was in a new world of music and writing after years of nothing mattering.

But when Kim burst into my life, it was even more empowering somehow than all of this new music that I was experiencing. They say that behind every great man, there is a woman. That was certainly the effect Kim had on me. But it would take years for me to figure that out fully, and by then, it was too late. Twenty years came and went just like that, and then I had Justin. My gift from a God I couldn't prove existed otherwise. And just as I was experiencing that gift of being a Father, my *own* Father, my biological Father, emerged out of nowhere.

My wife Michelle asked me about my biological Father, around 1999 and made me talk about it one night to the point where I cried. I had repressed feelings for years. I learned that it is okay and even good to cry sometimes.

"Dad," Justin asked me one day while I was driving him to school. "Yes," I said. "Do you think aliens believe in God?" He was eight years old at the time. He always asks me those kinds of questions when I am driving. I nearly forgot where I was going. "I don't know, son," I said. "Maybe." As a father, I learned it is okay to say, "I don't know." I said that a lot. Still do. You have to be honest and not bullshit. But most importantly, you have to be there. **"Father, you left me, but I never left you."** (from John Lennon's, **"Mother"**)

Justin was my life. And still is. We did everything together. And still do. And he is a funny kid. His kindergarten teacher told me "He makes me laugh every day!" He gets that from me. I have a wicked sense of humor. There was a time when he drove me nuts because all he would do was try to say something funny. Then he would say, "Is that kind of funny?" He was looking for approval from his Father, and his Father was a funny guy. Recently he told me, "When I grow up I want to be a doctor, or a lawyer, or a comedian." We make each other laugh every day. And when I make him laugh hard, to the point of him falling over hysterically, it is the best thing ever. And someday, when I am long gone, I know Justin will say, "My Dad was funny as hell!" That will be one of the things he will remember about me.

Justin and I were watching the movie **Spaceballs** one night when I got a call from my sister Tina that would end up being the catalyst to writing this book. She had gotten a message from our half-sister Teri. My long lost sister Teri had finally found us in 2012. It had been 35 years. It was amazing. I suddenly found myself talking to my sister whom I had never really known. The last recollection I had of her was when I was in the 4th grade, probably about 9 years old, and she couldn't have been much more than 4 years old. My sister Tina and I had gone to New Jersey to stay for part of the Summer with my Dad. I didn't know him either. My parent's split up when I was three, and I didn't know why. He was in the military. Army. Always had been, since aged 17. I was born in Washington, D.C. where he worked at the Pentagon. He went to Vietnam to set up communications systems in 1962. Before that, we lived for a brief time in Panama. I was about two and a half, three years old. I don't remember any of that, of course, but my mother told me some interesting tales. Apparently, I played with a spider monkey that was larger than me at the time and would pick me up and carry me around. I spoke some Spanish at the time. And I would play with large iguanas on the beach that must have seemed like dinosaurs to me. I only have a few memories of my father. And those were from mine and my sister's visit with him and his current family around 1968 in New Jersey. He had married a Chinese lady he had met in Vietnam named Lena. She had a girl named Christina already, and they had two daughters together, Teri and Debbie. I don't remember how long we were there, maybe a few weeks or more. But one day, Dad drove us back home to Missouri, and I would never see any of them again. Then, out of the blue, Teri contacted us.

Holy Shit! She had not forgotten us! She was curious and wondered how we were doing, I guess. I talked to her several times at length and we caught up on our lives. She put me in touch, eventually, with my father.

I started thinking about trying to find Kim again, and I mentioned it to Haans one July night during one of our frequent phone conversations. I didn't have internet at the time, so he started looking her up. With a name like Kim Jordan, it would not be an easy task.

I told Haans I wanted to write a letter to Kim, and asked him to see if he could find an email address for her. I remembered the conversation I had with Kim's Mother, saying she was in Germany, so Haans googled Kim Jordan, Germany and came up with something. There she was. Just like that. The next day at work, I looked her up online and sat in near shock as I read about what had become of her.

She had become a very successful businesswoman in Germany and Prague. And that is an understatement. She'd gone from Webster College to George Washington University for her Masters. Then later she went on to Harvard. Around 1990 or so she moved to Germany and eventually helped found a company. She must have done that shortly after I talked to her on the phone when I was on Martha's Vineyard.

The company became huge, and eventually she moved up to be CEO. Kim had climbed to the top of her field. I couldn't believe how big she had become. And among other things, she wrote an advice column on her own website for women about business. And through that web site, there was an email address. So I actually had a way to contact her. I could write my letter, and she might even read it. Maybe even respond! That was all I wanted to do. Just write her one more letter. I wrote it off the top of my head in about ten minutes. It had been 33 years since we were together. I basically knew what I wanted to say. It had been in the shoebox of my mind. It was just a matter of putting the words in order.

Dear Kim:

I've been waiting 33 years to write this letter and now that I have a contact for you I am not even sure where to start, so I will make it brief and to the point.

We broke up in 1980. Or rather, you broke up with me. We were kids, really. And although I was hurt and didn't understand it then, eventually I did.

I saw you again in 1986. We had lunch in Boston. And then, four years later, I talked to you on the phone, in 1990. You said you were getting married.

And that was it. Fourteen years later, in 2004 I think it was, I spoke to your Mother on the phone. She said you were the CEO of your own company in Germany and gave me your phone number. I think I tried calling you a couple of times but never got through to you. So here it is another eight years later…

Obviously I have thought of you from time to time over all these years. You were my first true love, and I guess I will never get over that. I realize the 21-year-old Kim Jordan is long gone. *But the purpose of this letter, really, is to let you know that I still and always will love you.* I knew Alice before the Looking Glass. And I would have followed her anywhere. Even Germany. You were an amazing person even then. Fiercely loyal, loving and ambitious. I always knew you would be successful, but your accomplishments far exceeded even my wildest imagination. Congratulations Kim. I am very happy for you.

I work for Express-Scripts in St. Louis, moved back here in 1993 from Martha's Vineyard. Got married in 2000. Separated in 2005 and finally divorced in 2010.

I have a ten year old "miracle" son named Justin. I am pretty much wrapped up in him. I will send you some pictures sometime. We adopted Justin; he was basically dropped in our laps. We weren't even looking to adopt. It just happened. We got him when he was 32 days old and have had him ever since. And I have to tell you, having a child is amazing. I never knew that kind of unconditional love.

Your professional life is very well documented and I have read a lot. I will read all of your columns eventually. They are amazing. Just great.

Are you still married? Did you have any children? How are your parents and your brother doing? I know they must have sold the house on Main Street in Wickford. I hope all is well with you. Please call me sometime. It would be great to hear your voice. Maybe we can stay in touch a little better than every 20 years or so!

Love,

Steven

P.S. You inspired a lot of songs over the years.

Most people only think about writing a letter like that. Some actually write them, and then throw them away. I not only wrote it, but actually sent it to her. It was therapeutic to me. Sort of a release. And I thought it might finally give me some closure. It seemed a bit crazy, even to me, but I did it anyway.

Every day I would go in to work like I normally do

and check my email. And every day, I would look for a reply from Kim. But of course, there was nothing. And I would talk to Haans about it and we would speculate. "Well Steve, you know she may just not want to hear about it," he said. "After all, that was a long time ago, and she lives in a completely different world now." "Yes, I know," I said, "but she is fundamentally the same person." I held hope that she would at least acknowledge that she received the letter. But still, day after day, there was no reply. I sent her a couple of more emails, and even left "the letter" and a few other shorter notes in the comments section of her advice column. Haans suggested that. "Maybe she just doesn't read the emails to that advice column," I told Haans. "She reads them," he said. She just wasn't responding. I sort of accepted that was probably the case, but at least I'd written and sent the letter and got on with my life as usual. Writing the letter felt good.

I was texting Haan's about writing "the letter," and he understood that it was good for me to write it after all those years, and he texted me something to the effect of "Get it all out! Blow it up!" And I texted back "Not blow it up, more like dissect and disassemble with care and respect." He responded, "Who wrote that?" meaning the line **"dissect and disassemble with care and respect."** "I guess I just did," I responded. Had he not said that, it would have blown by me. But now I had a good line having to do with my relationship with Kim as I see it now, so I had to do something with it. The next night, I wrote the poem and the following day, I emailed it to Kim.

I'm gratefully humble

For living today

Although you are so gone

From my life in any way

I took you for granted

Perhaps years ago

But appreciate you now

More than you'll ever know

I didn't understand then

The gift that was you

But now all these years later

I finally do

With care and respect

I will always love you

A lifetime of struggle

You come and you go

You were always inside me

I just want you to know

And when she tells you it's over

That she's not yours to protect
Dissect and disassemble

With care and respect

I hadn't written a poem, or a lyric as I call them, in years. But this summed it up quite nicely I thought. It represented precisely how I felt and what I wanted to say. For the first time in years, I had written something that I was happy with.

I hadn't gotten a response back from my letter, but I emailed it to her anyway. Not so much for her, but for me.

I thought about contacting her parent's again too, but times had changed. You can't call directory information and get a live person like in the old days. I didn't remember her parent's phone number. So I tried looking it up online, and there was no listing for Al Jordan on Main Street in Wickford. Something must have happened, I thought. And I was afraid whatever had happened wasn't good. My first thought was that one of them had passed away, and they sold the house. And for some unknown reason, I feared that it was her Mother. I don't know why I thought that. So I couldn't call her Mom and ask for Kim's mailing address in Germany. I just had to be happy that I had emailed the letter and the poem even though I got no response. Two months later, I finally got an email from Kim Jordan.

Hello,

I just wanted to let you know I just saw the mail. I honestly do not look at those mails too much to be honest, because I want to change askthealicegglass soon to another name and I am working on all the registrations right now. This mail will not be available after 31.8, but I do have your mail now.

I am glad to here you are well. Yes, my gosh it seems like a different life way back then. I am so happy for you and your son, and you sound happy, that is the most important. Sometimes years back in Missouri sneak in my dreams, I think everything in life has an influence on who you are. Those times influenced me.

I just sold Telecon and I am trying to start my next project. I want to turn Alice into a portal for women, but it is complicated and I need programmers. In the mean time I did take on another position part time with a company in Israel. Yes, the career Gods have been good to me but it has been a lot of work on the way, I must say.

I am married for the second time to a wonderful man he is German. We have a house in Dusseldorf and Prague. My father is not well at all he has Alzheimer and it is very difficult on my mom.

It is late here, I am currently in Spain for 3 weeks. I now have your address and will write you when I have all new accounts set up.

All the best thoughts,

Kim

August 24

I was right. Somehow, I guessed right. She didn't read that email much, she wasn't blowing me off, she had read "the letter," and she responded. And it was a positive response. I couldn't believe it. It was pretty amazing. My long shot gamble paid off. But I kept thinking, "I have nothing to lose," and by God, if you don't take the chance, nothing will happen. And not only had she sent me an email, she left me a couple of notes in the comments section of her blog, just as I had done for her. She posted those the very same day she wrote me that letter. And they speak for themselves.

Hello, I just saw all these mails, I sent a quick mail back for now. I am adjusting all these accounts, I was not ignoring you I honestly never read some of the comments because some people write really silly stuff sometimes. K

August 24

I just sent you a mail from my Czech address and it came back returned is the mail address here correct? I will go into Alice this week and send one from there I hardly ever use that because I am changing the name soon☺

August 24

Haans had to admit that he was wrong. She wasn't blowing me off. She read "the letter," and replied to it. Certainly, she lived in a different world, on a different continent, was married, and had essentially conquered Europe.

She read "the letter" and I got an

acknowledgement. Haans and I talked about how amazing that really was, but I had to tell him, I wasn't quite done yet. For some reason, I wanted more. It was less satisfying in the end than I expected it to be. The letter wasn't enough. I wanted to do more, to tell her more than what was in "the letter."

Haans asked me, "What is it that you want to tell her then?"

"Everything," I replied. "Everything."

The cemetery behind Lindenwood College is still there. The sports stadium overwhelms it in the background. I never cared for sports.

Chapter Eleven

What started out as a letter turned into a book. I didn't want to write this. I <u>had</u> to. It sounds crazy and obsessive, I know. But I figured it out after 35 years. Love is crazy and obsessive.

So I sat down one night and began writing, starting from the beginning. .

"I was late getting to the party because I worked the 3:30 PM to Midnight shift at Hussmann Refrigeration Company."

My long lost sister Teri was writing a book about the same time she got in touch with me this year. It is called **"Mending Broken Wings"** (published by AuthorHouse) and is based on her true story of having been abused as a child over a period of many years. When she published the book, it was a great inspiration to me. I had been thinking about writing a book for years. At first, I thought of writing a book about **The Eighth Day**. It would be called **"Band Out Of Time, The Story Of The Eighth Day."** That still may be written. And I wanted to write a book for my son called **"If I Should Die Before You Wake."** But getting in touch with Kim, and writing "the letter," changed the order in which I would write. The Kim story came first. And so I started thinking about writing again.

My sister getting in touch with me after all those years got me thinking about other people in my life that had meant a great deal to me whom I had lost touch with. It wasn't just Kim whom I tried to contact.

There was Annie. The beautiful blonde haired lady a few years older than me whom I had a crush on and friendship with at Lindenwood. I tracked her down on the internet. All I found for her was a mailing address, so I wrote her a letter. I explained how much our friendship had meant to me, and that I loved her. She never knew that. She wrote me a letter back, explaining that she really appreciated hearing from me, but that she was in a serious relationship. I think she misinterpreted the meaning of my letter. And understandably so. It's not everyday that someone gets a letter like that from an old friend from 30 years ago. And it's certainly not something I had ever done before.

And there was Julie. My dear Julie. All I could find for her was also a mailing address, so I wrote her a letter. I don't even know if it was her current mailing address, but I sent the letter anyway. It was an honest and emotional letter, but I was quick to explain up front that I was not trying in any way to interfere with her life or trying to "get back together with her." I just wanted to acknowledge how much she had meant to me at the time. I don't know if she ever got the letter. It was not returned to me as "not at this address" and I did not get a letter back from her. So it could be that it was the wrong address and the person at that address didn't bother sending it back through the postal system, or she could have read it and for whatever reason, decided not to reply back. I may never know.

I also contacted Janette and her sister Kim. And later, after the book was written, I wrote Jeannie Ickenbach a letter, but never heard back from her. As is the case with Julie, I don't know if I had the correct mailing address.

Then there was my Father. I had an email address for him. So I sent him an email. I deleted it, or I would include it here. I let him know how I was doing, and that I had a ten year old son named Justin. I credited him with me being a good father because he was not there for me, and growing up without a father made me realize the importance that having one is on a child. I never understood how he could disappear from his son's life. How could he do that? I hadn't thought about it in years. But suddenly I was thinking about it again. I felt abandoned all over again. Those repressed feelings came back in a wave one night, and I cried like a child again. I was finally confronting it. It took him two weeks, but he did reply to my email. He explained that it took him that long because he had to think about how to respond. It was not his idea, he said, to leave me. He had no choice. My Mother had served him with divorce papers while they were apart. He was in the army and we were stationed in Panama. My Mother took me and my sister back to Missouri and he went back home on leave between assignments to California. While he was there, he got the divorce papers. Then he had to go to VietNam. His family had effectively been taken away from him. It was not his choice. I never knew that.

One day my Father sent me and my sister this:

Hi, Steven & Tina:

Thought this was something to let you know, just something I remember from over fifty years ago:

First, for Steve, your son sounds like a guy who figures things out from scratch: would sure like to meet him, but let him know that I think he will go far in life!

In the middle fifties I was stationed with the US Army at Fort Kobe, the Canal Zone. You, Steven, was just a baby.

We decided one night to go to the Post Theater, where they were showing the movie "Giant". It has a lot of stars, including Elizabeth Taylor, Rock Hudson, and James Dean. The movie was three hours, twelve minutes and fifty one seconds long. The movie had no more than started when Steven got upset and started crying - screaming would be more accurate. I took my unhappy son out to the lobby, where we spent the remainder of the movie, waiting for it to complete. From that day until this day I never saw the movie. I downloaded it from the internet and just watched it this morning. It was good, but not "that" good.

If you haven't, Steven, you should watch it. Maybe you can figure out why you didn't like it, way back when.

Your Mom should remember this.

Love,

Dad

November 27

I thought it was a great letter. My sister ended up writing him back and opened up a whole different can of worms. I was moved when I read her letter to him and actually had to hold back the tears.

Dear Dad:

It's funny you should mention Ft. Kobe. My first memories are from Ft. Kobe. I remember the movie incident, don't remember the movie at all, but I remember you having to leave cause Steven wouldn't be quiet. Some twenty plus years later I was with my own family; Earl, Billie and Mary. At a place in Eureka Springs, Arkansas. There was an outdoor production there called "Shepard of the Little Hills", a moving and beautiful biblical play. Mary wouldn't be quiet there either and Earl had to leave with her. I had an instant flashback of that movie theater. Crazy the way our minds work. I have some first and lasting memories there to:

I remember our maid, don't remember her name. She spoke Spanish, therefore so did Steven. I remember riding with you to either pick her up or take her home. A jungle type place, crude, but a beautiful place. I remember thinking, "why doesn't she just stay with us in the room off the carport." It was a much nicer place. But then I realized it was her family there.

I remember being out and about and a cannon would fire, we had to freeze in our tracks and wait for them to play taps. Then I had to hustle home. That was my cue to go home. To this day, when I hear taps, I think it's time to go home.

I remember a party, a Halloween party I think, in a big barracks type building. It's the same building we took gymnastic lessons in, Mom went with me for those lessons and participated in some way.

I remember a neighbor who used to sit on his porch and eat the nastiest stuff I ever laid eyes on. Years later I figured out it was raw oysters on the half shell. He would take them out of a bucket, crack them open, drop hot sauce on them and suck them down! Yuck. To this day I can't even think about eating that snotty stuff, the texture is awful.

I remember another neighbor or friend of yours who had a pet monkey of some kind. This damn thing took Steven one time and wouldn't give him back. Scared me to death. And again, to this day, I won't go in the Monkey House at the St. Louis Zoo unless the kids absolutely insist. Little moneys ok, larger monkeys, no way!

I also remember school there. I had the notion that I was not smart because I didn't "get" things other kids seemed to pick up on easily. I felt stupid, I just didn't get it. It wasn't until second grade at Hancock Place Elementary that we learned I was nearly blind and need glasses. After I got glasses, things came easy to me too. There was a couple of years there that I didn't know what was going on though. Turns out I'm very smart ☺

I don't remember getting on an airplane, but I remember arriving in St. Louis and these people met us at the airport. Turned out to be Aunt Cona, Uncle Ralph and cousin Edna and her boyfriend Jim. Uncle Ralph carried Steve and Jim carried me. I watched Steve very closely, because I didn't know that guy who was carrying him, or me for that matter. This was a turning point in my life, because it marked the end of our life as a family; you, me, Mom and Steve. Even though I was a kid and didn't know what was going on at the time, I had a gut feeling that things were never gonna be the same again. And they weren't.

Anyway, those are a few of my first memories of my life. They started in Ft. Kobe, Panama.

Love,

Tina

November 28

What an amazing letter. I didn't remember anything from then. My sister is five years older than me to the day. We were both born on November First. And my parents were married on November First. And they broke ground on the building of Loretto Hall at Webster College, where Kim and I lived, on November First. Sure, it is all coincidence.

I had replied back to my Father's email with a simple thank you and told him I would like to include his letter in my book. It was the first time I mentioned to him that I was writing a book. I thought his story about the movie theater was great and actually very well written. His response back to me and my sister blew me away. To the max.

He replied:

Wow! This is a lot to disgest. First of all, for Steven: I would love to have a recent picture of you, since Tina assures me that you may be my look-alike at your age now. It may e a little too early for a face to face meeting yet, but I think it will happen eventually. But it must be there, not here. I have a lot of ghosts to chase, and all are there. Missouri & Arkansas. And my wife and children here are not a part of it. Now, about a book you are writing- I have, all of my life for as long as I can remember, wanted to be a writer. And when I retired from the Army in 1985 (?) don't remember exactly- I did write a book- took me several years, and I sent it to many, many agents until I finally found one who believed that she could sell it, and she did the best she could to find a publisher- and died of an unexpected heart attack. She had the only hard copy of the book and I have it on 4" floppy, written by a word processing program called "Enable". I cannot open the disk because I no longer have a copy of Enable. The title I gave the book is "Our Children, Lost", and is about the children in Vietnam, fathered by Americans, and left. The book is over 250 pages, and I hold a copyright on it. After my agent died I gave up on trying to market the book. Things are different now, self-publishing, etc. No one here is interested, so I may leave the copyright in your hands- you may be able to read the floppy. I no longer have an interest in getting it published- so long ago, no one cares. Now, Tina: I am astounded that you remember all of that about our time at Ft. Kobe.

About the maid- I no longer remember her name either, but you are right on- she lived with all her family members in a one room thatched house on the edge of the jungle. Dirt Floor. But all she knew. And we did have a maid's room in the carport. When the cannon fired in the evening, it was called "retreat". We all stopped and saluted as the flag was lowered for the evening. If we couldn't see the flag, we faced in that direction. I don't *remember the party, but the neighbor who ate the oysters was my first sergeant, and I sometimes joined him in eating oysters. The monkey- he was actually a monkey my friend and neighbor brought with him from the states- God knows why, since there were plenty already there- but anyway, the little bastard stole my sun glasses and never did give them back to me! Also had a neighbor who had an anteater. Remember that? I'm surprised you didn't mention the bicycle- remember that? If you don't I will you about it.*

Love you both-all

Dad Thomas

November 28

"Wow!" is right! So that's where I get it from. . .

And here's another coincidence: My Father was the same age as I am right now when he started writing his book. We were both the same age when we started writing our first book. When he started writing **"Our Children, Lost"**, I started managing **The Eighth Day** and moved to Martha's Vineyard. That was the same year I saw Kim again. Life is filled with coincidences, I guess. I call it magic. Twenty-five years after seeing

Kim for the last time, I started thinking about this book.

"I need to write all of this down," I told Haans. And the idea that Kim herself might actually end up reading it motivated me even that much more. That was my audience, I thought. I wouldn't worry about a mass audience. Just like with the songs on **"boyfriend."** "If I could get her to read this book, that would be great," I thought. It is my story, as old as humankind. But it is her story too. It sounds crazy and obsessive, I know. **But I figured it out after 35 years. Love is crazy and obsessive.** I talked to Haans about the book many times. "But what is the point?" Haans asked. It took me awhile to answer that. I wasn't even sure myself. Then it came to me in words and not just in emotions. It is the story of enduring love. "What is the upshot?" Haans asked. That's it. Enduring love. I had to wait all this time to tell her that I wasn't kidding. I still loved her. It is sort of like saying "I told you so! I told you that I loved you," and I had no better way of proving that point but to write this book after all these years. It's not complicated.

It was time, I thought, that I tell Kim I was writing a book. I'd been working on it for almost four months. I had no idea how she would react to that. And, I told her, not only did I want her to read it, but also I asked her to contribute to it if she felt so compelled. I thought that was only fair. So I sent her an email explaining it all. I would change the names and addresses if it ever got published, I said. A week or two went by, then finally I got an email from Kim.

Hi,

I have no electric right now I am in USA and we got hit bad, I will get to you soon. I am dealing with the storm and my dad Alzheimer, Cam moved to east coast, I will respond when I have constant e-mail. K

Kim was in Wickford to be with her parents for the Storm of the Century they named Sandy. By the time I found this out, Sandy had already come and gone, wreaking havoc on the east coast. It was very tempting to call her parent's house, but I knew they had a lot going on with the clean up after the storm, so I didn't. Kim knew I was writing this book by then, and said she would respond, so I just continued writing and waiting for her to answer back.

In the days that followed that awful storm, I was thinking about Kim being back in Wickford. And I asked myself, what do we really have in common after 33 years? We live on the same planet, I thought. That's about it. Then, a line came to me. **"As long as we are both alive, we will share the sky."** "That's a good line," I thought. "I have to do something with that." I wrote it down. Later that evening, I completed it. Sometimes that's just how it happens. I get one line and the rest sort of writes itself.

I sent that poem to a few people, including Kim and my sister. My sister asked, *"Who wrote that?"* You know you have something good when they ask "Who wrote that?" Every girl that I showed that lyric to reacted similarly. They all loved it. I was writing again. And doing a pretty damn good job of it.

While looking through some of my notebooks to see if there had been something else I had jotted down that related to the book I came across a lyric my son Justin had written. He was a writer too. And this poem struck me as interesting.

I'm 7 Years Old

I'm 7 years old

My heart is stone cold

Got my hands in the music and my feet on the floor

My Daddy yells "come right here son"

Then he says "let's have a rap battle one on one"

I won then he yells at me

Well I'm a green mean rapping machine

He's not 7 years old

His hearts stone cold

He don't got his hands in the music

But his feets on the floor

And my son Justin has written other things too, but I will let the kid write his own book. I just thought that it was cool that he would be writing about being seven years old, period. Write away kid! Justin is an artist. He can draw and create in that way better than I ever could. And I will let him read this book someday, and that may influence him too. I believe all kids are artistic by nature, and then they suck that out of you. Rules do that. Life does that to people. If we let kids rule the world, things would be a lot different. John Lennon said first we have to liberate the women, then when that is done, we have to work on *children's liberation*. I explained to Justin last year the meaning of "hypocrite." That is what grown ups sometimes become. You have to be honest. Grown-ups are hypocrites. Not all of us, but in general, that is true. Kids have no rights. And that is fucked up. Kids have an imagination and see things in an innocent way, and I try to hang onto that. Just today, I was talking to Justin on our way to my sister's house for Thanksgiving. We were talking about light and mirrors, how mirrors reflect light and can change its course. I told him about Leonardo DaVinci, and that he once worked on a project to make things invisible by using a series of mirrors to bounce light around an object. Without light, DaVinci figured, you could not see the object. He thought if he could bend light, it would render that object invisible. I believe he figured out that it wasn't possible to bend light, but still, he gave it a shot! Justin understood. And then he said, "If there were no light, there would be no darkness." "Damn," I thought, "that's pretty good." Justin has my gift for abstract thought and reasoning. He is an artist, like his old man. And that is not necessarily a genetic trait, but environmental.

Some people see a squiggly line, but in that line, I see a face, an expression, and emotion. I guess that's what they call interpretation. We all see things differently. And that's just a squiggly line. Imagine how complicated it can be with men and women living together. When you're twenty! Women are like cats and men are like dogs. That's about all I know about it. Squiggly lines. Different meanings. I would have died for Kim. I just never drew that squiggly line. Or she didn't see it. And if I had, she probably wouldn't have understood it.

Kim knew I was writing a book but I hadn't gotten a response back from her about that so I sent her yet another email.

My Dear old friend:

Well, we're not old, but you know what I mean!

Hope all is well. I know you are very busy. How is the portal going?

I am on chapter ten of my book. I have an editor now, but I just gave her the first eight chapters and she has not started on it yet. I hope to be done by Christmas, but rewrites may go on awhile.

I wanted to assure you that before I even think about publishing this, I am going to change the names, business names and addresses, etc. so no one will know it is you that I am writing about.

I will not even mention the type of business you are (were) in so no one can put it together. Not that I am writing anything bad about you, to the contrary actually. But still, I want to protect your privacy.

I was thinking, it takes you a long time to respond to me, and I realize how very busy you are. I check my email everyday, hoping to get some big long detailed letter from you. But haven't heard anything since you were in Wickford, October 31st. I would still like your input. As much as you care to write. You are a good writer, Kim. Anyway, I was thinking it might be easier to actually mail you a copy of the entire book on disc when I finish it. That way you will have the whole thing in context.

So please send me your mailing address when you can.

Thank you and I hope you are well.

Best Wishes Always,

Steven☺

November 16

She obviously didn't check her email very often, I knew that, but I was growing increasingly impatient with the lack of feedback from her. But to my surprise, I got this email from her the very same day:

Hello:

I am sorry. I was in Wickford and survived the hurricane, than Israel just had bombs, my biggest customer, it has been crazy. Can you use the mail address girltaletalk.com that would be better and I answer more. I am back in Prague this weekend so I will have time to read everything if you can send it to me again it would be cool.

Thanks I am in a little craziness now after leaving Israel. K

It was great news. Unbelievable almost. Kim apparently wanted to read "the book." So that Friday, I emailed her the first draft of the first four chapters. If you remember, Dear Reader, that takes the story up to my historic visit to her parent's house in Wickford, R.I. in 1979. The chapter ends with "This story was just beginning..." I thought it would be enough to send her to make her want to read the rest. And I was right. She responded via email the following Sunday:

Hello,

What I can say is that your talent for writing and for words has not changed, I would keep writing. The details are a nice narrative touch which I think will make a difference. I understand when you are done you will replace the names with other ones but as you write you can not do that or you will distance the story. I think you have talent for words and writing, I really do not have a lot to say and it is probably better if I wait until it is finished to read it.

K

November 18

It was an encouraging letter. "I would keep writing," she said, and so I did.

I'm still not sure why Kim danced down the isle of life with me as far as she did before pulling back. I guess it was because she was young and hadn't figured everything out quite yet. She was young and naive and she loved me, I know that. She hadn't yet developed who she really was and what she really wanted. She felt like she really needed me. Then at some point realized she didn't. I am finally okay with that. She turned into the beautiful and successful women that I always knew she would become. I read all of her articles on her website with great interest. And I found out a few tidbits about her personal life in the process. She didn't get married again until after she was already a CEO. I don't know what happened to her first marriage, but I am guessing it had something to do with her moving to Germany. Her future husband was a supplier to her company. So they met and developed a relationship through business. And she said, "it happened by chance." You can plan your education, and to an extent, your career. But you can't plan love. It just happens. And I thought it was great that she was writing columns for women about business. Ironic, but I was straight into feminism well before Kim was in my life. John and Yoko taught me that when I was about twelve years old. I would meet Kim seven years later.

Kim learned a lot of lessons in life after me. Especially about how difficult it is for women in business. I talked to my Mother about that, and she understood what Kim must have gone through. She faced the same prejudice and "boys club" mentality during her career at McDonnell-Douglas in St. Louis. It's interesting that my Mother also immediately understood why I felt I had to write this book. I didn't have to explain it to her at all. And she remembered some things that I had forgotten. She told me how Kim picked up baby Mary when she was fussing in the courtroom during that stupid drug bust and took her outside. And that Kim was wearing pink clothes that day. "How do you remember that?" I asked. "I don't know," she said. "But I remember it very vividly. It's just one of those things that has stuck in my mind." Some things stuck in my mind too, while others came slowly to the forefront. My sister recalled something that may seem a bit trivial, but I found fascinating. Tina remembered that baby Mary was the first baby that Kim had ever held. "How do you remember that?" I asked. "Because when she picked Mary up, and Mary was only a couple of weeks old, she said 'this is the first baby I have ever held,'" she answered. And she said it was Kim who influenced her daughter Billie to pursue dancing. She explained that Billie went to the St. Louis High School For The Performing Arts because of Kim. I didn't realize the effect that Kim had on my niece Billie. My family loved her. My Mother had kept a small wooden sculpture that Kim had made at Lindenwood. It was about twelve inches tall, and sort of looked like a mushroom with a hole in it. To be honest, it looked like a penis with a big hole in it, to me. I didn't know what it meant, but it was cool as hell. She must have made it in art class. It was made of wood, shaped, sanded, stained, varnished and had her name on the bottom. For some reason, my Mother gave me that sculpture back around 1999. I was living with Michelle and we were planning to get married. One day Michelle asked me who made it, and I told her. She didn't like the idea of me having a piece of art made by my first true love, and asked me to get rid of it. I told her no, that I couldn't do that, it would be bad karma. And I really believed that. ***"Instant Karma's gonna get you. Gonna knock you right in the head. Better get yourself together darlin'. Pretty soon you're gonna be dead."*** (John Lennon from **Instant Karma**) She ended up throwing it out without me knowing it. Our marriage didn't work out in the end. Maybe I was right about that karma thing. I wish I had that sculpture today. It was the only physical thing I had left of Kim Jordan.

My Mother also recently told me what those cool wrap around skirts were that Kim had. Turns out those skirts Kim showed me in her dorm room at Lindenwood were dance skirts. Just regular, standard dance skirts. I had never seen anything like that before and I just didn't put it together. Kim lived in dance clothes. And probably had since she was a child. But in many ways, she was still a child when I fell in love with her. ***"We were kids, really"*** is what I wrote her in "the letter." **"Yes, my gosh it seems like a different life way back then,"** she had replied. And it certainly was. So much time, so many changes. But I still knew Kim. I could recognize her writing, her phrasing, her motivations, her career and how and why she got what she wanted. Some things never change. Like those lyrics I wrote way back then.

Looking back on it, I still think this is a brilliant line:

"She took my synonyms

Eating peanut M&M's"

Since I have been writing this book, it dawned on me that they still sell peanut M&M's and I buy them occasionally and of course think of those days back then with Kim. Like feelings, some candies never change.

I have been thinking about Kim's Mother, Jan Jordan, a lot lately while writing this book. Kim told me her father is suffering from Alzheimer's and it is very hard on her Mother. I can't even imagine. It has been eight years since I talked to her Mother. I am tempted to call her. But I wouldn't know what to say. I envied Kim's parents. We could have been like them. Happy and married forever.

My old high school journalism class friend, Mike Snelling, died in a car crash in 1982. Mark Snow and I went to his funeral. I remember thinking, "man, that could have been me." And I thought about Kim's older brother.

I never wrote any songs for Julie. I don't know why. I didn't write then. I am not sure why now. It somehow seemed pointless.

Kim had an amazing career, and like she said, she worked hard for it. She also sacrificed a lot. More than she will ever know, really. When I think about all of the sacrifices Kim unknowingly made, of course, I think of me. And I think of

The Beatle's song **"And Your Bird Can Sing."**

Look up the lyrics sometime and you'll see why.

Another amazing coincidence occurred as I was writing the last few chapters of this book. Haans told me that Deana Tucker, my old high school journalism classmate, was organizing a book signing party for Miss Veita Jo Hampton, our journalism teacher. Miss Hampton had written a novel called **"August In Defiance."** (Bluestocking Press). As it turns out, she had written several books over the years, including poetry books that were highly acclaimed. I got in touch with Deana and told her I would be there. I hadn't seen either of them in 35 years. The same evening of meeting Miss Hampton, I took Justin to see Paul McCartney in St. Louis. He was only doing two shows in the USA. St. Louis and Houston. And I kept it a secret from my son who we were going to be seeing. He didn't know who it was until Paul waked out on stage. "Oh my God!" he said, over and over. So I met with Miss Hampton and saw Paul McCartney all in the same day. November 11. I'll never forget it. And Justin will remember it for the rest of his life.

Because this book is an autobiography, and therefore non-fiction, I couldn't embellish on the facts. Make us vampires, and this might be a best seller.

But I can imagine living with Kim when we are retired at 141 Main Street, Wickford. We are walking, holding hands, down Main Street, a quarter inch of snow on the ground. She slips, and I grab her waist. We laugh and she asks, "Do you love me Steven?" "I will always love you, Kim" I reply. "I will never leave you." And she says, "Well, how much do you love me Steven?" I say "I love you to the max!" She laughs contently.

No one ever loved her like I do. And after all these years, after reading this book, she finally knows that. We continue on down the street, carefully, sweetly, the winter wind blowing slightly from the northeast. I can see us living together in that house when we are 64 and beyond. Just as we were when we were twenty. That would be magic. It could happen. It is not impossible. And I still believe in magic. If we had married when we had planned to, we would be married for 30 years now.

I can write about what I think, even if it didn't happen. And I can write lyrics. And I am very excited about doing more of that after this book. I have more writing laying in wait. And I am only 54 years old. I can imagine meeting a woman and falling in love again. I know that will happen. She may be reading this book right now. The one thing I can say about myself in all honesty, is that I am loyal. I don't take love for granted. I value friends and family more now than ever. There's a line from the movie **"The Wizard of Oz"** that comes back to me. **"You are not judged by how much you love, but how much you are loved by others,"** or something like that. I am happy and very optimistic about the future. I kept thinking about the song **"Some Enchanted Evening"** while writing this book. And I realize it may seem silly or strange or overstated depending on who is reading this, but that doesn't matter to me. You can believe what you want. And it may come true.

Some enchanted evening

You may see a stranger

You may see a stranger

Across a crowded room

Once you have found her

Never let her go

Once you have found her

Never   let   her
go!

I wrote one more lyric for Kim 33 years after our relationship ended. But it will not be the last, I am sure. And like everything else about our story, it came from down in the basement and into the sky.

There Are Many Fine Fronts In Dusseldorf

It's such a long long way

To Wickford today

The promenade

Of the River Rhine

Loretto Hall

When she was mine

Bidding time

Drinking blue nun wine

But as long as we are both alive

We will share the sky

There are many fine fronts

In Dusseldorf today

Wickford Cove and the Gardner's wharf

Tailor-Wibbel-Lane

The gaslights flicker

The same today

I WAS A DRUMMER SHE WAS A DANCER

Having coffee in the twisted tower of Schlosstusum

Just before the sunset colors come

But as long as we are both alive

We will share the sky

Down Pleasant Street

St. Lambertus Church

Young Cemetery

Old Narragansette Church

Gas lights flicker on the streets

To greet the evening incomplete

But as long as we are both alive

It's such a long long way in life

We shall share the sky

We shall share the sky

Epilogue

Pantoniq played his drum high atop a tall hill that overlooked the valley separating his village and the river below. It was 451 AD and many tribes traveled the pathway there. But at dusk, there would be few. He loved the view, and the calm of the air. The smell of hundreds of bonfires from his home to the east. And the rushing water one hundred and fifty feet beneath him seemed to accompany his rhythm. He was 19 years old and a fisher by trade. But just before dark, he was a lone drummer. He drummed for his own pleasure. It gave him solace and peace in an otherwise harsh existence of fishing and survival.

Then one night, a tiny figure appeared just beneath the hill. It was a beautiful young girl he had never seen before. Her figure cast shadows across the field and into the shimmering river below. The moonlight and the stars were magic that night. And she began moving, slowly at first, as he drummed. Was she dancing? It took him a moment to figure it out, but yes, she seemed to be dancing to his drumming that echoed into the night. To be sure, he would stop playing. And she would stop dancing. When he began again, she began again. He looked upon this girl reacting to his drumming with pure joy and amazement. And then, just as quickly as she came, she disappeared into the night. The same thing happened the following night, and the night after that. His drumming had purpose now. He got better and better, and as his drumming did, so did her dancing. Then one night, she wasn't there. "She will be back tomorrow," Pantoniq reassured himself. So every evening, he would go to the top of the mound and play and wait for his dancer. Days turned into years. His drum skin was stained with blood from his fingertips, but he never stopped looking for his dancer.

November 18

About the photographs:

I had been thinking about going back to Webster and Lindenwood to take photographs to accompany this book. I hadn't been to either place in I can't tell you how long. It had been many years. I thought photos of the actual places might be a good addition. But I also realized it might be emotional for me. So I finally planned it just a couple of days prior to actually going and doing it. It was Saturday, December 8th. It didn't dawn on me until I was driving home from work the night before that the date was also the 32nd anniversary of the assassination of John Lennon. I didn't plan it that way, it just happened. So that was strange, I thought. And I went alone. I had to Mapquest directions on how to get to Webster. The highways had changed a lot in 33 years. On my way there, I turned the radio on, and a Billy Joel song came on. **"A Matter Of Trust"**. It is a very powerful love song, and I damn near cried. But I was determined to do this and not get too teary eyed, so I pushed onward. When I got to Webster, not much had changed. It was pretty much just as I remembered it. And it was a bit eerie. I found Loretto Hall, where Kim and I lived. There was a man walking by and I asked him if it was open. No one else was around. He said "I don't know, it is administrative offices, but you could try the door. Webster Hall is open though, you can wander around in there!" I walked up the fourteen steps to Loretto Hall, and it was closed. But it was amazing to see the place again. And to my surprise, I did not feel sad. To the contrary, I felt good! I walked all around the two buildings and took photographs. It was a somewhat dreary day, not a lot of sunshine and a bit cold. Not a cloud in the sky. Yet, not overcast either. So in the photos, the sky is pure white. Not blue, just white. I did go into Webster Hall, and there were only a couple of people there. No one questioned who I was or why I was there. I just walked around taking it all in.

Then I went to Lindenwood and did the same thing. I walked around the whole campus unnoticed and took photos of several of the key buildings. It was an amazing feeling. But again, it was not sad. It was very cool, actually. I was very happy I did it. And I think having those photos in the book is important. I couldn't help but email Kim the following Monday to let her know. "I wish you could have been there," I said, in describing my experience. So these are the photographs and that is the story of me taking them on the 8th of December.

Steven M Thomas

The Lyrics

(in order of appearance in book)

Cardboard Box Tomb

Before I Fall

Most Of My Money

Real Big Deal

Mirror Of Mistakes

A Lover And A Friend

Girls Go On

Now

Shades Of Blue

Underground

Dinoland

The Individuals

Only If You Cared

Talkin' On The Telephone

Sleep Sweet

Nothing Valid

The Trouble With Love

Call Me Back

I Know A Song

Sweet Attraction

With Care And Respect

Lonely Dance Step

There Are Many Fine Fronts In Dusseldorf

My Love Speaks From The Sky

(not mentioned in the book, written after the book was done)

Despite Life

(not mentioned in the book, written after the book was done)

Note: I had lost all of these lyrics on paper over the years. Every last one of them that are included here came from my memory, except for Cardboard Box Tomb, which my friend Eric remembered. There were many more that I forgot. And four new ones that I wrote during the course of this book.

Cardboard Box Tomb (year written unknown)

I'm still in love with
The rug on your bedroom floor

I still can't go into the dorm room

We shared before

You put me me down with the

Things I couldn't see

I almost died from

Losing your love

Carefully recorded

All I thought of

Like horror from hell

Heavy torment and gloom

I placed every page

In a cardboard box tomb

Before I Fall (1978)

I'm standing on the edge of love

I just don't know which way to jump

Without you I seem so damn small

I can't seem to balance on this ball

So push me girl before I fall

Please push me girl before I fall

I'm somewhere in the line of success

I just don't seem to show my best

And without you I just can not talk

I can't live and I can not walk

So push me girl before I fall

So push me girl before I fall

Please push me girl before I fall

I'd kill myself you know I can't

A murder's cool but suicide aint

You see a murder is forgivable

So do this for me I implore

Please push me girl before I fall

Please push me girl before I fall

Most Of My Money (1978)

Couldn't afford it
Bought it in six packs

(I don't think that I'll be coming back)

Just living

I'm walking lonely railroad tracks

(I don't think that I'll be coming back)

Just living

So kiss my picture on the wall

I'm in a state of mental pause

And I've

Already given you

Most of my money

I hope they don't think I'm a chump

(I don't think that you have been a chump)

For trading

I've invested everything on this dump

(I don't think that you have been a chump)

It's fading.

Accountant says he's no regrets

I'm winging it for cigarettes

And I've

Already given you

Most of my money

Real Big Deal (1978)

Your future's getting brighter

Your headlines getting higher
While calling people liar

With your sex appeal

You say that how you look is

How you feel

But how you feel

Is like a wheel

So roll away

How does it feel

To consider yourself to be
A real big deal?

(most of the other lyrics to this song were forgotten, forever blowing in the wind)

<u>Mirror Of Mistakes</u> (1978)

When you get old, old, old

The difference that age makes

Like when you get slow, slow, slow and slow
Forget that my heart aches

When you get low, low, low

Forget that my heart breaks

I'm only looking through, through, through and through

Your Mirror of mistakes

Year of mistakes year of mistakes

If you just knew, knew, knew

Forget what your love takes

And when you feel low, low, low

Forget what your love makes

I'm only looking through, through, through and through

Your Mirror of mistakes

Year of mistakes

A Lover And A Friend (1978)

You haven't known me long

But it's been long enough to know

In case you haven't noticed

I love you

But you say things you don't mean

Do you mean to be so cruel?

You've taken me for granted

I played the perfect fool

And loved you

I loved you

Don't you know I loved you?

Many nights ago

Cold and still alone

So this is where it ends

For a lover and a friend

I loved you

Don't you know I loved you?

Out of touch with feelings

Out of hand

Didn't have it planned

I am staring at ceilings

Empty hand

Didn't have it planned

So this where it ends

For a lover and a friend

She's changing her mind

Like I'm changing my scene

She's a classy looking school girl

I WAS A DRUMMER SHE WAS A DANCER

On the cover of Seventeen magazine

Girls go on

Girls go on and on

We break down

They just shake down

And go on and on

She's moving so fast

I wish I had the time

But she won't let me love her

She don't even know her mind

Girls go on

Girls go on and on

We break down

They just shake down

And go on and on

Lolitta

Did I have to me ya

You know I can't defeat ya

Girls always win in the end

Girls go on

Girls go on and on

We break down

They just shake down

And go on and on

<u>Now</u> (1978)

The things I've seen and done before

Don't seem to matter anymore

I'm different now and so are things

Names and dates all change

But when you see me staring off

And wonder what I'm thinking of

It's doubtful that I'm in the past

Vague memories through the broken glass

If it's in past my mind is in

And you're wondering where I've been

I'm looking back at where I've been at

I'll come around and in a minute

Now

Now is more important than then

Then is just a past tense of when

And that is less important when through

Cause now I wanna be with

You...

Shades of Blue (1978)

Walking for no reason but to think of you

Singing in no particular scheme

So I may dream of you

Launching into outer space

So I may see your shinning face

Don't want to be away from you

In shades of blue

Sitting in the driver's seat

But I'm not there

Lost in familiar faces as they

Stop to stare

Catching up on my sleep

My eyes they must be ten feet deep

Don't want to be away from you

In shades of blue

<u>Underground</u> (1978)

They came back in a Cadillac

Drove on down to their part of downtown

How oddly the people worried

How funny they scurried

And questions and rumors flew around

That these men were disrespectful

It was, they were but they weren't protesting

Yet they seemed disgusted

So they soon got busted

Now it's time to move on down

To the underground the underground the underground the underground

Take your time with life

It's so easy

It's so dreamy when you're underground

They can't afford no brand new ford

Twisted and confused they were half spoken

Yet under this justice

The gavel did speak

Sensationalism and

Questionable doubt

So they had to let them go

They let them all out they had to let them all out!

Ha ha ha!

Take your time with life

It's so easy

It's so dreamy when you're underground

Take your time with life

It's so easy

It's so dreamy when you're underground

You're under ground.

Dinoland (1964)

Dinoland

Dinoland

Oh what a place to be

Where the trees are small

Dinosaurs are tall

And the distance is far away

To Be

I took my girl out for a date

In my daddy's car

We hadn't driven very far

When we saw a dinosaur

I said that's

Dinoland

Dinoland

Oh what a place to be

Where the trees are small

Dinosaurs are tall

And the distance is far away

To Be

Dinoland is a happy place

A happy place to be

So everyone go to Dinoland

Go there and be free

<u>The Individuals</u> **(1972)**

We're All Individuals

We're all not alike

If you act as each other

We'll go on strike

We're all very different in many ways

We're all different characters

In our own plays

But no matter what happens

Through thick and thin

We'll all be individuals

To the end

Only If You Cared (1973)

Do you know what you're doing to me?

Or are you at all aware

That I love you

And I'll be true

Only if you cared

Can't you see what I feel for you?

Or is it that you're just scared?

Cause I love you

And I'll be true

Only if you cared

If I heard after you moved

That you liked me just a bit

I tell you that would be it

I'd search everywhere

Only if you cared

Do you know what you're doing to me

Or are you at all aware?

Cause I love you

And I'll be true

Wishing you had cared

Only if you cared

Talkin' On The Telephone (1973)

Talkin' on the telephone

To myself

Talking of my riches and my wealth

Yes, my wealth

But I am just a poor boy

And I think that you should know

That I just been talking to myself

On the telephone

Whenever you feel angry

Don't throw sticks and stones

Instead try talking to yourself

On the telephone

Sleep Sweet (1979)

Close your pretty eyes

Relax your weary mind

Lay down on the bed

And I'll sooth your aching muscles

Sleep sweet

Sleep sweet

Listen to this lullaby

And I'll love you in the morning

I'll love your till I die

Nothing Valid (1979)

Smoke hung in the air

Down in the basement

I pitter ponder

Whoops and wandered

Wondering what tomorrow would bring

Settling in a chair

Less in appearance

But quite aware

I coaxed myself

Opened myself another beer

The little things you said and done

Come rushing back

Into my head

I break into a grin

And try your phone again

But can't catch up to you

It's been such a long time

I find myself and try myself
To write damn near

Anything valid

Nothing valid at all

The Trouble With Love (1981)
Notes on the door

Babes in the bookstore

Moments of silence

For ladies in waiting
Dressing to choice

For casual dating

Give it all up

Romantic scenes

Designer jeans

Moments of violence

For gentlemen drinking

Moments of quiet

He sits contemplating

Notes on the door

The trouble with love

<u>Call Me Back</u> **(1981)**
If your whole world lets you down

And you want my love around
Call me back

I'll be back

I'll come back

To you

If your love turns bittersweet

You could run away with me

Call Me back

I'll be back

I'll come back

To you

Sometimes love finds
Lifetime listless

Blowing kisses

To the air

Anytime that you find

Love life lonely

Call me only

I'll be there

Someday it may all come back

I could have a heart attack

Call me back
I won't be back

Then no one would bring me back

To you

I Know A Song (1981)

I know a song

Won't make you mine

But I just can't write a letter
So play along

And you may find

That it really could be better

I knew a song

As a child

That got right to my head

But as a man

I write no songs

To make you change your mind instead

I know a song

Won't make you mine

But I never did expect it

So play along

And you may find

That you may not regret it

I know a song, oh!

I know a song, oh!

I know a song!

Sweet Attraction (1978)

Upstairs to the attic
She hides her childhood toys

Her life's been filled with static

I WAS A DRUMMER SHE WAS A DANCER

Since she's focused on the boys

So hide your face in makeup

And tie your new wool sweater

You know you need protecting if you can't

Do anything better than that!

Sweet Attraction

I'm talking satisfaction

Sweet Attraction

That's in you

I haven't seen nothing new!

So then she's cool surrounds herself

With all that laughter

She's taking a winner

Out for dinner and knowing

What he's after!

Sweet Attraction

I'm talking satisfaction

Sweet Attraction

That's in you

I haven't seen nothing new!

With Care And Respect (July 19, 2012)

I'm gratefully humble

For living today

Although you are so gone

From my life in any way

I took you for granted

Perhaps years ago

But appreciate you now
More than you'll ever know

I didn't understand then

The gift that was you

But now all these years later

I finally do

With care and respect

I will always love you

A lifetime of struggle

You come and you go

You were always inside me

I just want you to know

And when she tells you it's over

That she's not yours to protect

Dissect and disassemble

With care and respect

Lonely Dance Step (1980)

She took my synonyms

Eating peanut M&M's

A backrub for my favorite dancer

I guess I'm just a strange romancer

I'm just a lonely dance step

You can pick me up in two or three steps

You performed me before

You should know me by heart

When shall we start again

There are many fine fronts in Dusseldorf (Nov 7, 2012)

STEVEN M THOMAS

It's such a long long way

To Wickford today

The promenade

Of the River Rhine

Loretto Hall

When she was mine

Bidding time

Drinking blue nun wine

But as long as we are both alive

We will share the sky

There are many fine fronts

In Dusseldorf today

Wickford Cove and the Gardner's wharf

Tailor-Wibbel-Lane

The gaslights flicker

The same today

Having coffee in the twisted tower of Schlosstusum

Just before the sunset colors come

But as long as we are both alive

We will share the sky

Down Pleasant Street

St. Lambertus Church

Young Cemetery

Old Narragansette Church

Gas lights flicker on the streets

To greet the evening incomplete

But as long as we are both alive

It's such a long long way in life

We shall share the sky

We will share the sky

My Love Speaks From The Sky (Dec 3, 2012)

My love speaks

from day to day

Reciting silent poetry

I see her eyes

What no one sees

Casting spectrums of

academy

What words just

Can not own

And whistling through

The bus lined streets

An image slowly matching me

In spite of all

The energy

Their faces stand alone

In bluish traces from

A thread

The clothes give image

To the head

Despite the novelty, they're dead

What the needle pricked

It has not sewn

The passing clouds

Envision things

I WAS A DRUMMER SHE WAS A DANCER

And tumble slowly

Over me

The wise man looks

But doesn't see

The prophecies above his

Head and home

The world spins like

A penny

Escaping more than many

Deflecting love and pitty

Like the money

Passing through your bones

My love speaks from the sky

On cold nights

When trash blows by

She stays too busy

To ask me why

Never knowing what

The clouds may bring

Despite life (Jan 15, 2013)

You wake up in the morning
Pour yourself a cup of coffee

Get on with daily glory

The grind and push of business boring
And years repeat themselves

Ever engaging

Numbers changing

When you are alone

You are still by yourself
And love and childhood

Seems like someone else

Despite life

You are someone else

Because of life

You are someone else

Than when you began

And you never understand

I WAS A DRUMMER SHE WAS A DANCER

Despite life

STEVEN M THOMAS

I WAS A DRUMMER

SHE WAS A DANCER

STEVEN M THOMAS

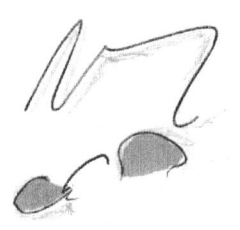

Drummer Dancer Publications

Other books by this author:

Chase The Rabbit

Rabbits Never Die

The Hollywood Murders

Aloha, Logosi!

Goodbye Harlow Nights

STEVEN M THOMAS

Made in the USA
Middletown, DE
09 February 2020